CW00549757

QUESTIONS AND ANSWERS ON
IMMIGRATION TO BRITAIN

QUESTIONS AND ANSWERS ON IMMIGRATION TO BRITAIN

Farid Raymond Anthony

Barrister (England and Wales) (non-practising)
Barrister and solicitor, notary public, commissioner for oaths
(Republic of Sierra Leone)
Barrister and solicitor of the Republic of the Gambia
Member of the Honourable Society of the Inner Temple
Member of the Immigration Law Practitioners' Association
Member of the Joint Council for the Welfare of Immigrants

FRANK CASS
LONDON • PORTLAND, OR

Dedicated to my wife Joan and to my children

First published in 1996 in Great Britain by
FRANK CASS & CO. LTD.
Newbury House, 900 Eastern Avenue,
London IG2 7HH

and in the United States of America by
FRANK CASS
c/o ISBS, 5804 N.E. Hassalo Street,
Portland, Oregon 97213-3644

Copyright © Farid Raymond Anthony 1996

British Library Cataloguing in Publication data
A catalogue record for this book is available
from the British Library

ISBN 0-7146-4272-X

Library of Congress Cataloging-in-Publication data
A catalog record for this book is available
from the Library of Congress

All rights reserved. No part of this publication may be reproduced in any form, or by any means, electronic, mechanical, photocopying, recording or otherwise, without the prior permission of Frank Cass & Company Limited

Printed in Great Britain by
Bookcraft (Bath) Ltd, Midsomer Norton, Avon

Contents

Acknowledgements

I wish to thank my wife, Joan, and our children who pestered me to continue my legal career or do something along the same lines to keep my mind active and alert (as a result of which I set up the Immigration Advisory Services of Kent). My thanks also go to my wife for helping with the checking of the manuscript for the inevitable spelling and typing errors. I also wish to thank His Honour Judge Eugene Cotran (editor in chief of the Butterworths Immigration Law loose leaf service) immensely for looking through my manuscript and making suggestions, and for writing the Foreword to this book.

My thanks also go to Desmond de Silva Q.C., head of chambers at 2 Paper Buildings, Inner Temple, and an old friend in whose chambers I started reading immigration law. This was where I became interested in the subject. I thank Adrian Jack, my 'pupil-master', who did not discourage me from doing anything not connected with criminal or civil law.

Regrettably, due to a life-long practice in my own chambers abroad, practising in a fused system, I found the split system of practice in the United Kingdom inconvenient, time-wasting and more costly, and so set up a consultancy. I wholeheartedly support those colleagues who are advocating a fused system in Britain!

The Immigration Advisory Services of Kent has been instrumental in getting the manuscript off the ground.

I thank all those who in one way or the other have made this publication possible.

Finally I thank Frank Cass & Co. Ltd for publishing this book.

Abbreviations

AC: Appeal Cases
All ER: All England Law Reports
BDT: British Dependent Territory
BNA: British Nationality Act
CIO: Chief Immigration Officer
CMLR: Common Market Law Report
CTA: Common Travel Area
D of E: Department of Employment
EC: European Community
ECO: Entry Clearance Officer
EEA: European Economic Area
EU: European Union
FCR: Family Court Report
HO: Home Office
HOPO: Home Office Presenting Officer
HX/(number): Hatton Cross hearing centre and reference number of the case
Imm.A.R.: Immigration Appeals Report
IAT: Immigration Appeals Tribunal
IO: Immigration Officer
NHS: National Health Service
QBD: Queen's Bench Division
SSHD: Secretary of State for Home Department
TA: Temporary Admission
TH/(number): Thanet House hearing centre and reference number of the case
TLR: Times Law Report
UNHCR: United Nations High Commission for Refugees
WLR: Weekly Law Reports

List of questions

1 General

1. What is an 'ECO' and what is 'entry clearance'?
2. What is an immigration officer (IO)?
3. What is the difference between a High Commission and an Embassy?
4. From which countries are citizens 'Commonwealth citizens'?
5. Which countries are British dependent territories (BDTs)?
6. Which countries are 'visa countries'?
7. Are there any exemptions from the visa requirements for visa nationals?
8. Do those not designated as 'visa nationals' still need entry clearance to come to the United Kingdom?
9. When is entry clearance not mandatory?
10. What are 'leave to enter' and 'leave to remain'?
11. When can entry clearance or leave to enter be refused?
12. Once entry clearance has been obtained by an individual before leaving his home country, will he be examined or interviewed again on arrival at a port or airport in the United Kingdom?
13. What is 'limited leave'?
14. What is 'indefinite leave to remain'?
15. Is registration with the police normally imposed on every foreign entrant?
16. What is 'settlement'?
17. What is meant by 'right of abode'?
18. Does everyone need a sponsor before applying to come to the United Kingdom?
19. Who are considered as 'parents'?
20. Who are considered as children for immigration matters?
21. What if I overstay the period granted me?
22. What is the 'common travel area' (CTA)?
23. When I enter the common travel area would I need a permit to travel from the country that I entered to any of the other countries in the CTA?
24. Having entered United Kingdom lawfully, can I then travel freely to other countries which form the European Union – the United Kingdom being part of the European Union?
25. Which countries form the European Union?
26. Can any other type of British passport entitle free entry to the United Kingdom?
27. What are the immigration rules?
28. Apart from the rules what other legislation, orders or rules are there relating to immigration?

29. To whom does an applicant who has been refused entry or other applications appeal?
30. Who are adjudicators?
31. What is the Tribunal?
32. What is judicial review?
33. Are there time limits for an appeal to be brought?
34. If leave to enter is refused can a person get temporary admission (TA)?
35. What is variation of leave and curtailment?
36. Do Commonwealth citizens have to register with the police in the United Kingdom? How is registration carried out?
37. What is meant by 'public funds'?
38. What is meant by 'adequate accommodation' and 'exclusive accommodation'?
39. What is meant by maintenance?
40. What is a 'prohibition' on, or a 'restriction' from, employment?
41. What is meant by 'close connections' with the United Kingdom?

2 Visitors

42. How long can a visitor be allowed to stay in the United Kingdom?
43. Do all arrivals need entry clearance?
44. If a visit is sponsored who makes the application for entry clearance?
45. What are the requirements for a visit?
46. Apart from the above, will I have to show a reason for visiting?
47. With regard to accommodation and maintenance, will the visitor have to show that he can do both by himself?
48. What form does the 'intention to return' test take?
49. What do I have to do to show that I intend to return?
50. Can a visitor transact business during his visit?
51. Can a visitor apply to extend his stay?
52. What are the conditions or requirements for a permanent stay if a visitor gets married?
53. Generally can a visitor change his status during his visit?
54. What happens if a visitor arrives without an entry clearance and is held at the airport until a decision is taken to admit or refuse him entry?
55. Apart from ordinary visits are any other 'types' of visit permitted?
56. What is the position if a visit is for the purpose of medical treatment?
57. If visiting the United Kingdom for medical treatment will six months be the maximum period that will be granted?

3 Professional workers

4 Students

5 People entering on business

6 Working in the United Kingdom

256. Do the same rules apply to British citizens who have been away for over two years?
257. What if a person who claims entry as a returning resident is given leave to enter for a limited period?
258. Who may become holders of special vouchers?
259. What are the benefits of having a special voucher?
260. Can a special voucher holder bring his spouse and children to join him?
261. Are there any concessions granted for someone to settle after long period of residence in the United Kingdom?
262. In all the cases of settlement mentioned above what effect will settlement have on the citizenship of the persons who have settled?

9 Asylum

263. Who is an asylum seeker?
264. Who determines the application?
265. What rules govern the granting of asylum?
266. What happens to the applicant when he makes the application?
267. What is exceptional leave to remain?
268. What is the policy towards granting settlement to one with exceptional leave to remain wishing to bring his family to join him?
269. What is 'well founded fear of persecution'?
270. What is meant by 'a particular social group'?
271. What if there has been a previous application in another country?
272. Can the wife and children and dependants of an applicant be included in the application for asylum?
273. Can children apply for asylum if they are not accompanied by parents?
274. Can a person apply from overseas for asylum in the United Kingdom?
275. What is meant by 'safe third country' and 'links with the United Kingdom'?
276. What are the Convention and Protocol relating to the Status of Refugees and which countries are signatories to them?
277. What is the position of those running away from civil war?
278. Can someone with dual nationality seek asylum in the United Kingdom?
279. Can an asylum seeker, or someone granted refugee status, or other applicants travel abroad?
280. Can asylum be transferred from another country to the United Kingdom?

10 Offences and deportation

281. Is illegal entry an offence?
282. Who is an 'illegal immigrant'?
283. What will be the result if deception is used to enter or remain in the United Kingdom?
284. What may amount to deception?
285. Is it also an offence to assist someone to enter the United Kingdom?
286. What other offences are there relating to immigration?
287. Are there any offences that carriers are liable to commit?
288. Can a court sentence anyone to deportation?
289. When does a court recommend deportation?
290. When is someone liable to a Home Office deportation?
291. Can an appeal be made against deportation?
292. Is there anyone who cannot be deported?
293. What factors are taken into account before a deportation order is made?
294. Can anything be done after an appeal has failed but before the order to deport is made?
295. When the head of a family is deported will every other member of the family also be deported?
296. What happens after a deportation order has been signed?
297. Can a deportation order be revoked?
298. What is the difference between a deportation and a removal?
299. When is bail given?
300. Who may grant bail?
301. How is bail applied for?
302. Can bail be opposed?
303. If bail is granted, what next?
304. Can a person let out on bail be arrested?

11 Appeals

305. Who has the right to plead before the adjudicators or tribunal?
306. Are there people who have no right of appeal?
307. Where there is a right of appeal how long will the appellant have to bring the appeal?
308. What are the stages of appeal?

12 British nationality

309. Does having indefinite leave to remain make a person a British citizen?
310. Can a person become a British citizen and still keep his original nationality?

311.   Which law governs British citizenship?
312.   What is a British overseas citizen?
313.   Has a British overseas citizen the right of abode in the United
        · Kingdom?
314.   What is a British protected person (BPP)?
315.   What are the means by which British citizenship can now be
        obtained?
316.   What are the requirements to obtain citizenship by birth?
317.   What are the requirements for naturalisation?
318.   When an application for naturalisation has been approved is a
        passport then sent to the applicant?
319.   How does one qualify for registration?
320.   What if the absence from United Kingdom of an applicant who
        applies for either naturalisation or registration is longer than
        allowed?
321.   What was a British visitor's passport?

Cases mentioned

Foreword

by His Honour Judge Eugene Cotran, LL.D*

Many books have been written on UK immigration law and practice since it became a growth subject some 25 years ago. This work is of a different kind and is welcome for several reasons. It is in 'question and answer form', the first such book in the field of immigration law. The questions are well selected and the answers concise and to the point. The coverage (there are over 300 questions and answers) is extensive, complete and thorough. The arrangement follows the sequence in the latest immigration rules (HC 395 of 1 October 1994) and has parts on general matters and definitions; visitors; students, businessmen and the self-employed; representatives of overseas firms; writers, composers and artists; investors; retired persons of independent means; work permits and employment in all its categories; matters relating to the European Union and the European Community; settlement (including marriage, children and other relatives); asylum and refugees; illegal entry, deportation, offences, appeals and bail. The answers are in simple English and happily use the old discursive style which appeared in the old immigration rules (HC 251) rather than the style of the new rules (HC 395) which are drafted more like a statute or statutory instrument.

Although the book is primarily intended for use by the lay immigrant, it is certainly a useful starting point for the student and the professional adviser since it will refer him or her to the general principles of immigration law and practice, whether derived from the immigration Acts or immigration rules, or landmark cases decided by Tribunals, the High Court, Court of Appeal or the House of Lords.

With regard to professional advisers, immigration law is perhaps the only branch of law in England where persons other than barristers and solicitors give day-to-day advice to immigrants. This book will be a most useful guide to all of them, whether at law centres, or immigration welfare organisations, or asylum and refugee organisations, or whether they are immigration law consultants.

The author, Mr Farid Anthony, has the highest qualifications and experience for writing this book. He is of Lebanese origin and is a citizen of Sierra Leone, married to a British Citizen. He was called to the English Bar (Inner Temple) in 1963 and then practised as a solicitor and barrister in Sierra Leone and the Gambia for some 28 years.

During that time he was associated with the Commonwealth Chambers at 2 Paper Buildings (Sir Dingle Foot QC, then Sir Charles Fletcher-Cooke QC, then Desmond de Silva QC, and myself) and helped the members of Chambers tremendously with the intricacies of the laws and procedures in west Africa, with its various peoples, when the Chambers did much work there.

In 1992 he came to live in Britain and spent about a year at the same Chambers to obtain a Certificate of Practice in England. He devoted much of his time to immigration law and practice, one of the leading specialities at 2

Paper Buildings. In 1993 he set up an immigration law consultancy, the Immigration Advisory Services of Kent, in Gillingham (Kent), with an office in London.

With his considerable experience of Commonwealth immigrants and of immigration law and practice, it is not surprising that Mr Farid Anthony has produced an excellent book which will be invaluable to laymen, students, and to all immigration law advisers, whether they be professionally legally qualified or not. I commend it to them all as essential reading.

Eugene Cotran
22 August 1995

---

*Circuit Judge; Visiting Professor of Law, School of Oriental and African Studies, University of London; Former Law Commissioner and High Court Judge, Kenya; General Editor of Butterworths Immigration Law Service.

Introduction

This book is written for easy reference and is intended for those who want to discover facts about immigration requirements in the United Kingdom for themselves, whether they contemplate coming to Britain for limited periods or otherwise. It is also intended for those who are already in the United Kingdom and who want to find out whether they can extend their stay or be allowed to remain permanently and settle. Immigration advisers and lawyers will also find it useful for quick reference purposes.

The questions and answers in this book will help potential immigrants keep within the new rules that came into effect in October 1994. It is very strongly advised that readers should adhere to these rules. They should never try to enter Britain surreptitiously; they should ensure that they are seen by an immigration officer and the appropriate travel document is stamped.

There are two sections. Chapters 1–11 deal with immigration matters and Chapter 12 deals with matters pertaining to those who are not British citizens but who have settled in the United Kingdom and wish to apply for British nationality.

It is not possible to present an in-depth study of immigration within the scope of a reference book like this. Immigration is a complex issue and those interested in the study of immigration law and practice will have to refer to additional sources. This work does, however, give an overview of the requirements before entry, on entry, and after entry.

The reader must bear in mind that it is becoming increasingly difficult to emigrate to the United Kingdom, or even to come to the United Kingdom on a temporary basis. The rules are being made tighter by the day. The answers given here are based on the rules applicable at the time of preparing this book – HC395 – but it will not be surprising if, from time to time, the rules are amended. The likelihood is that they will become harsher than the present ones. There is, for instance, a tendency for the authorities to 'equalise' conditions for males and females, where requirements differed between the sexes in the past, by making the more difficult rule apply to both sexes (instead of the less difficult condition). For instance if a rule discriminates between a man and a woman by giving the woman more advantages, then the tendency is for the rule to be changed in such a way as to reduce the advantages for the woman rather than granting the man a more advantageous position. Before the new rules came into effect in October 1994, a widowed mother seeking to join her daughter was allowed to do so but a widower had to be 65 or over. Under the new rules this advantage was taken away from widows and the age requirement was 'equalised' to require them both to be 65 or over. It must be granted that the authorities have tried to remove discrimination between male and female, although this removal, as stated, has, in more instances than not, been disadvantageous. (One example of the few exceptions to this trend is that, under the former rules, the foreign wife of a male student could join her husband in the United Kingdom but the foreign husband of a female student could not join his wife in the United Kingdom except subject to certain conditions. Under the new consolidated rules female students have been put in the same position as males regarding their spouses.)

Another aspect to be taken into account is that, with the European Union now standardising rules for the various member countries, a stage will soon be reached where refusal of entry into one EU country will mean refusal of entry into all of them.

It is not difficult to note that the majority of refusals are against nationals of poor Third World countries who, it is felt, want to come to the United Kingdom to reap the benefits of a welfare state that gives free education, free medical treatment, free housing, and pays them if they are unemployed or ill. Things are rapidly changing and these 'free' services are proving to be very expensive these days and are difficult to obtain, even for those settled here.

Very recently the Social Security (Persons from Abroad) Miscellaneous Amendment Regulations 1996 came into operation. This removed the right to claim housing benefits, income support and council tax benefits from those seeking asylum as well as others. See the postscript for more on this. Furthermore, there are two bills in progress in Parliament which will further restrict benefits to foreigners seeking asylum and even to some British citizens. These are the Immigration and Asylum Bill and the Housing Bill. Great opposition has been encountered from immigration advisers, Church leaders, social workers and many other bodies but so far they have not proved very effective. The regulation already in place is being opposed in court but a decision has not been reached at the time of writing.

In the section about the 'working holidaymaker' readers will find that, although a child can now be admitted with the parent in this category, the age limit for the child is set at five years. The most probable reason for this is that, in the United Kingdom, a child should start school at this age and, as State schools are free, the rule will mean that the child of the holidaymaker will not be able to remain in the country for this type of benefit.

Those who wish to come to the United Kingdom are advised to think deeply about their reasons for wanting to come here, particularly if they are reasons other than a short visit to relatives, or to see what the country looks like, or for a course of study that is not available in their own country, or if they have a wife or family already settled here. Whatever reasons readers might have for coming to the United Kingdom, I am sure that this book of questions and answers will point out the main requirements that need to be satisfied. It is not exhaustive in its answers and an adviser or expert on immigration should be consulted on any matter which may need in-depth advice.

Wherever reference is made to 'he' in a general way, please read it to mean 'he or she'.

In order to enable the reader to understand the terms used, I have decided to begin with general questions.

A set of numbers after a case signifies the case number in the adjudication hearing.

Chapter 1

General

Chapter 1 contains questions and answers based on generally used terms that will enable the reader to understand the immigration rules.

Q.1   **What is an 'ECO' and what is 'entry clearance'?**

A.   'ECO' means 'entry clearance officer'. These are officers in overseas countries, stationed either in the British Embassy, High Commission, or a similar diplomatic post, who are responsible for checking and interviewing an applicant and granting or refusing him entry clearance *before he leaves his home country.* ECOs are normally stationed in non-visa Commonwealth countries; in visa countries they are called 'visa officers' and grant visas. Entry clearances and visas serve the same purpose and are generally used interchangeably although the term 'entry clearance' is often used whether a visa or entry clearance is involved. A visa, entry certificate, or any other such document, according to the immigration rules, is to be taken as evidence of the holder's eligibility for entry to Britain even though he is not a British citizen, but it does not include a work permit.

Q.2   **What is an immigration officer (IO)?**

A.   He is the official at a port or airport in Britain who decides whether to let you in and what conditions to impose, depending on his interview with you. His powers are controlled by the immigration rules.

Q.3   **What is the difference between a High Commission and an Embassy?**

A.   High Commissions differ from Embassies in that Commonwealth countries have High Commissions and non-Commonwealth countries have Embassies, but they both perform the same duties abroad.

Q.4   **From which countries are citizens 'Commonwealth citizens'?**

A.   All British citizens are Commonwealth citizens and so are citizens of the following countries: Antigua and Barbuda, Australia, Bahamas, Bangladesh, Barbados, Belize, Bermuda, Botswana, the British Virgin Islands, Cameroon, Canada, Cayman Islands, Cyprus, Dominica, Fiji, Gambia, Ghana, Gibraltar, Grenada, Guyana, Hong Kong, India, Jamaica, Kenya, Kiribati, Lesotho, Malawi, Malaysia, Malta, Mauritius, Montserrat, Mozambique, Namibia, Nauru, Nevis, New Zealand, Nigeria (suspended), Pakistan, Papua New Guinea, Pitcairn Island, St Kitts, St Lucia, St Vincent, St Christopher and Nevis, Seychelles, Sierra Leone, Singapore, Solomon Islands, South Africa, Sri Lanka, Swaziland, Tanzania, Tonga, Trinidad and Tobago, Tuvalu, Uganda, Vanuatu, Western Samoa, Zambia, Zimbabwe.

Q.5   Which countries are British dependent territories (BDTs)?

A.   Under the British Nationality Act 1981, the following countries became BDTs: Anguilla, Bermuda, British Antarctic Territories, British Indian Ocean Territories, Cayman Islands, Falkland Islands and dependencies, Gibraltar, Hong Kong (until 1997), Montserrat, Pitcairn, Henderson, Ducie and Oeno Islands, St Christopher and Nevis, St Helena and dependencies, the sovereign base area of Akrotiri and Dhekelia, Turks and Caicos Islands, and the Virgin Islands. Some of these territories are also Commonwealth countries.

Q.6   Which countries are 'visa countries'?

A.   Citizens of certain countries are designated as 'visa nationals' and need a visa before coming to the United Kingdom for whatever reason. Some of these countries are also Commonwealth countries and are marked with an asterisk (*): Afghanistan, Albania, Algeria, Angola, Armenia, Azerbaijan, Bangladesh*, Belarus, Benin, Bhutan, Bosnia-Herzegovina, Bulgaria, Burkina-Faso, Burma, Burundi, Cambodia, Cameroon, Cape Verde, Central African Republic, Chad, China, Comoros, Congo, Cuba, Djibouti, Egypt, Equatorial Guinea, Eritrea, Ethiopia, Gabon, Gambia*, Georgia, Ghana*, Guinea, Guinea Bisau, Haiti, India*, Indonesia, Iran, Iraq, Ivory Coast, Jordan, Kazakhstan, Kenya*, Kirghizstan, Korea (North), Laos, Lebanon, Liberia, Libya, Macedonia, Madagascar, Mali, Mauritania, Moldova, Mongolia, Morocco, Mozambique, Nepal, Nigeria*, Oman, Pakistan*, Philippines, Romania, Russia, Rwanda, Sao Tome e Principé, Saudi Arabia, Senegal, Sierra Leone*, Somalia, Sri Lanka*, Sudan, Syria, Taiwan, Tajikistan, Tanzania*, Thailand, Togo, Tunisia, Turkey, Turkmenistan, Uganda*, Ukraine, Uzbekistan, Vietnam, Yemen, all the countries of the former Yugoslavia (not including Croatia and Slovenia), Zaire.

Nationals of countries marked with an asterisk are known as 'semi visa nationals'. Although they require entry clearances to enter the United Kingdom they are regarded as Commonwealth citizens for other purposes and can enjoy whatever privileges remain to such citizens, such as not requiring registration with the police. All persons holding passports or documents from the former Soviet Union and the former Yugoslavia, all stateless persons, and those holding non-national documents, require visas. There is no discretion to grant leave to enter to a visa national who does not possess a valid current visa.

From time to time, countries may be deleted from or added to the above list. For example, Sierra Leone was added on 21 September 1994 due to an influx of asylum seekers to the United Kingdom from that country. It is always advisable to check the list from the Embassy/High Commission in your country. Carriers (airlines and ships) have a duty, under The Carriers' Liability Act, to ensure that all passengers to the United Kingdom have a valid entry clearance or visa where so required, and carriers are subject to a fine (of £2000 per passenger) if they do not comply with this legislation.

Q.7 **Are there any exemptions from the visa requirements for visa nationals?**

A. Yes. There are certain circumstances exempting such requirements:

(i) People who are settled in the United Kingdom and who do not stay away from the United Kingdom for longer than two years. These qualify for admission as returning residents (although they are visa nationals) and do not require a visa.

(ii) People who were given leave to remain in United Kingdom for longer than six months, such as students, work-permit holders, or people staying for some other long-term purpose, and who have gone abroad and are returning within the period of the leave granted, do not need a new visa. Those who had six months or less will have to have a visa – visitors, for example.

(iii) Those holding refugee documents issued by countries that are signatories to the 1951 Convention, and the Council of Europe Agreement 1959 (abolishing visas for refugees), if coming for visits of three months or less, do not need visas.

Q.8 **Do those not designated as 'visa nationals' still need entry clearance to come to the United Kingdom?**

A. There are certain circumstances in which they will need an entry clearance. The new rules state that 'a visa-national and any other person who is seeking entry for the purpose for which prior entry clearance is required ... must produce to the immigration officer a valid passport or other identity document endorsed with ... entry clearance' and quite a few categories have now been included as requiring entry clearance for work or settlement; the list is:

(i) people coming for permanent settlement (irrespective of which country they are coming from – whether commonwealth, non-visa, or visa countries);

(ii) people coming for work experience or training. A work permit has to be obtained beforehand. No mention is made of entry clearance. Those coming to seek employment, it seems, do not require entry clearance but will need a work permit, although entry will be easier with entry clearance. Their spouses will need entry clearance;

(iii) working holidaymakers and their children, even if they come from Commonwealth countries, will now (under the new rules) need an entry clearance to enter in this capacity;

(iv) teachers/language assistants and their spouses and children;

(v) representatives of overseas newspapers, news agencies, and broadcasting organisations and their spouses and children;

(vi) representatives of overseas firms and their spouses and children;

(vii) the private servants of diplomats and their spouses and children;

(viii) overseas government employees may either obtain an entry clearance or produce satisfactory evidence of their employment with the overseas government on applying for entry to the United Kingdom. It appears that their spouses and children will need entry clearances;

(ix) ministers of religion, missionaries, or members of a religious order, and their spouses and children;

(x) airport ground staff working for overseas-owned airlines, and their spouses and children;

(xi) persons with United Kingdom ancestry (even if they are Commonwealth citizens) and their spouses and children;

(xii) businessmen, people who are self-employed, investors, writers, composers, artists, and their spouses and children;

(xiii) those with rights of access to children resident in the United Kingdom;

(xiv) British overseas citizens may seek either an entry clearance for indefinite leave to enter or may apply for a special voucher overseas;

(xv) retired persons of independent means, and their spouses and children;

(xvi) adopted children from overseas;

(xvii) parents, grandparents, and other relatives (see paragraph (i) of the answer to this question).

In effect the only categories not requiring mandatory entry clearance are those from non-visa countries travelling as visitors, visitors in transit, people visiting for medical treatment, students and prospective students, and au pairs. The rules, nevertheless, provide for optional entry clearance if you are not a visa national. This course of action will prevent delay at the point of entry. It must be noted, however, that if application is made for this optional entry clearance and it is refused, but the applicant still travels to the United Kingdom, entry will probably be refused as passports are usually marked indicating refusals. Where the IO is unaware of this refusal and it is not disclosed, this may amount to illegal entry on grounds of non-disclosure as shown in question 11(xv) below.

Q.9 When is entry clearance not mandatory?

A. Those who do not need mandatory entry clearance are people from non-visa countries which are not mentioned in question 8 and those who are mentioned in the answer to question 7. As stated in the answer to question 8, the only categories not requiring mandatory entry clearance are, in effect, those from non-visa countries travelling as visitors, visitors in transit, people visiting for medical treatment, students and prospective students, and au pairs.

If you do not need entry clearance you can choose to get an optional one. The advantages of this are that you are less likely to be refused entry on arrival and, if you are refused, you can appeal from within the United Kingdom. Visitors, prospective students, and students on courses of less than six months' duration without an entry clearance have no right of appeal. The disadvantage is that if you apply for an optional entry clearance from abroad and are refused it will be harder to obtain entry later unless the circumstances leading to the refusal have changed. (An appeal from abroad is possible.)

Most people who do not need a visa or entry clearance just arrive in the United Kingdom and, so long as they can satisfy the immigration officer at the port of entry that they can comply with the various requirements for the category under which they are entering (a visitor or student, for example), they are likely to be admitted. This is not always successful, however, and it has been known for some to be turned away. If someone can satisfy the IO here, he should be able to satisfy the ECO in his own country and so reduce the risk of losing the fares he paid and having a stamp in his passport indicating that he has been refused entry. The new rules provide that 'any person who wishes to ascertain in advance whether he is eligible for admission to the United Kingdom may apply for the issue of an entry clearance'. The applicant can decide whether he wishes to exercise this option.

Q.10 What are 'leave to enter' and 'leave to remain'?

A.   These terms refer to permission given by the immigration officer in the United Kingdom to the person seeking entry at a port or airport to enter or remain in the United Kingdom for a given period of time. If, after the completion of an examination by an immigration officer, notice of granting or refusal of leave to enter is not given within 24 hours then it is deemed that leave to enter for six months has been given. The conclusion of the interview is where there is only one interview and the immigration officer decides not to have a second interview (*R v SSHD ex parte Labiche* (1990) Imm.A.R. 157), or at the conclusion of the last interview (*R v SSHD ex parte Thirkumar* (1989) Imm.A.R. 402).

Stamping the passport will be taken as giving notice of granting leave but where the passport is stamped and the period granted is illegible it will be deemed to be for six months from the date of entry (*R v SSHD ex parte Minton* (1990) Imm.A.R. 199).

Q.11 When can entry clearance or leave to enter be refused?

A.   There are certain grounds, under the rules, where the entry clearance officer (in the overseas country) or the immigration officer (in the United Kingdom) will refuse clearance or entry according to the rules. These include circumstances where:

(i) entry is sought for a purpose not covered by the rules;

(ii) a deportation order is in force against the applicant;

(iii) the applicant is not in possession of a valid passport or other document showing his nationality and identity;

(iv) there is a lack of proof that someone entering United Kingdom with an intention of travelling to other common travel areas will be allowed to enter those areas;

(v) the applicant is not in possession of an entry clearance and he is a visa national (see questions 6, 7 and 8);

(vi) where the Secretary of State has personally certified the applicant as undesirable for the public good;

(vii) where a medical officer confirms that it is not desirable to admit the applicant for medical reasons (for example, where the applicant suffers from a contagious disease) – unless there are strong compassionate grounds to allow him in.

Other grounds where the immigration officer may refuse entry are given as:

(viii) failure to furnish information to enable the officer to decide whether to grant entry or to decide the conditions to be satisfied if entry is granted;

(ix) failure of returning residents to satisfy the rules for entry by such persons (see the section on returning residents);

(x) holding a passport or identity document of a territory not recognised by United Kingdom or which does not accept British passports;

(xi) failure to observe time limits or conditions set for leave to enter or remain;

(xii) obtaining previous entry by deception;

(xiii) failure by the applicant to show that he will be admitted to another country he proposes to visit after leaving the United Kingdom;

(xiv) failure by a sponsor to give an undertaking, if so required, to take responsibility for the applicant's maintenance and accommodation;

(xv)   making false representations or failure to disclose any material facts for the purpose of obtaining a work permit; whether such representation is known to the applicant or not (for example, if made by a prospective employer). Similarly, any false representation or failure to disclose material facts in applying for leave to enter will have the same effect;

(xvi) in the case of a child under 18 travelling without his parent or legal guardian, failure to provide, if required, written consent of the parent or guardian for such child to seek entry. This does not apply to a child seeking asylum;

(xvii) refusal to undergo a medical examination when required by the immigration officer;

(xviii) conviction in any country of an offence punishable by 12 months or more imprisonment (if such an offence carries less than 12 months outside the United Kingdom but would have carried 12 or more months' imprisonment in the United Kingdom then this would fall within the net; an exception on strong compassionate grounds can be considered);

(xix) where, in the light of information received about the character, conduct or association of the applicant, it is conducive to the public good to refuse entry to the applicant.

Leave to enter or remain may be refused in some of the cases above even where entry clearances have been obtained.

Q.12.   **Once entry clearance has been obtained by an individual before leaving his home country, will he be examined or interviewed again on arrival at a port or airport in United Kingdom?**

A.   The 1988 Immigration Act provides that, where a passenger has leave to enter prior to arrival, he shall not be subject to examination as provided in the 1971 Act but may be examined only in order to establish his identity. This applies if he arrives within seven days of permission to enter being granted and only to his first arrival after permission is granted. Thereafter he may be subject to examination but it is not likely to be rigorous.

        If it is found that he obtained the entry clearance by deception he will be refused entry. False representation or non-disclosure of material facts in applying for entry clearance from the home country may also result in refusal, as will a change of the circumstances that enabled the applicant to obtain clearance in the first place, except in the case of children whose age exceeded 18 after applying and obtaining entry clearance. Here, the applicant will have a right of appeal and can stay until the appeal is determined. The IO will have to state the reasons for such refusal and justify them at the appeal.

A time will be set for the person's removal at the time of the refusal and the IO will ask if he wishes to appeal. The appeal form should be lodged immediately and the removal directions will be cancelled pending the appeal. The IO is not precluded from hearing fresh representations to see if the applicant can satisfy the requirements of the category applied for. These grounds are mentioned above (question 11 (viii–xix)). Appeals in such cases are mostly lost.

If the person says he does not wish to appeal then he will be given a form (IS102) to sign and removal is most likely.

Q.13 What is 'limited leave'?

A. Permission to enter or remain will have a time limit and certain other conditions – for example, 'leave to enter for six months – employment prohibited' may be stamped on the entrant's passport. This is distinct from 'indefinite leave to remain'.

Q.14 What is 'indefinite leave to remain'?

A. This is stamped on an applicant's passport when he qualifies for settlement and applies for and is granted settlement. It means that the holder has no limitation to the period of his stay in the United Kingdom. He is not subject to any conditions for staying. He is, however, subject to a limitation on the period for which he may be absent from the United Kingdom (see returning residents). Application should be made only after certain periods of lawful continuous residence in United Kingdom and each period will be shown under the relevant headings in this book. This period is generally four years. Marriage to a British citizen may also result in an application for a change of category to that of 'indefinite leave to remain (settlement)' to be granted, provided all the rules relating to marriage are satisfied. See question 52 for an outline of these rules which apply in every case.

Q.15 Is registration with the police normally imposed on every foreign entrant?

A. Normally all those over 16 years of age, in the following categories, who are granted limited leave to enter or remain, are required to register under the rules:

(i) those entering for employment for more than three months except those in permit-free domestic employment in diplomatic households, or ministers of religion;

(ii) those entering for longer than six months as students, prospective students, au pairs, businessmen, self-employed people, investors, persons of independent means, creative artists, and family members of EEA nationals who are themselves not EU nationals;

(iii) spouses or children of those required to register with the police;

(iv) where an extension is granted that brings the category within the list of those required to register as mentioned above (except where the person is under 16, or a minister of religion, or a private servant in diplomatic household employment, or is the spouse of a person settled in the United Kingdom).

Q.16   What is 'settlement'?

A.   The Immigration Act 1971 s2(i)*(c)* mentions those with right of abode as (inter alia) those who are 'ordinarily resident' but this has been amended by the British Nationality Act 1981 which defines settlement as applying to those who must be ordinarily resident and who have permission to remain permanently.

This is where, as shown in a previous answer, a person who has been in the United Kingdom legally (or has been permitted to enter or remain lawfully after entering unlawfully), who is given indefinite leave to remain, and who is ordinarily resident in the United Kingdom. To obtain settlement there are required periods of residence in United Kingdom (see under each category) – generally four years, but one year if the applicant is married to a British citizen or someone with settlement status. In the latter case, certain rules mentioned above will have to be satisfied (see under the answers dealing with marriage and settlement below). Usually, apart from the stamp on the passport, a letter from the Immigration and Nationality Department will be sent to the applicant telling him that there is no longer any restrictions on the period he may remain in the United Kingdom, that there is no longer any need for permission to take up or change employment, and that if he leaves the United Kingdom he will normally be readmitted for settlement provided certain conditions are satisfied (see the answers dealing with returning residents below). A child born to him in the United Kingdom since 1 January 1983 who is not a British citizen may now be entitled to be registered as such, and any child born to him here whilst he remains settled may be a

British citizen automatically at birth. This is subject to the condition that the parents are married, otherwise citizenship can only be derived from the mother. Settlement does not mean that the applicant has acquired British citizenship. He may remain settled for ever and remain a citizen of his original country without applying for British citizenship. (See questions and answers dealing with citizenship below.)

Q.17   What is meant by 'right of abode'?

A.   All British citizens have this right and it need not be stamped on their passports, but it is also a special right available to Commonwealth citizens who were born before 1 January 1983 and had one parent born in the United Kingdom. It is also available to a woman who is a Commonwealth citizen and who was married before 1 January 1983 to a man born in the United Kingdom or to a man who had been registered or naturalised as a British citizen, or was married to a Commonwealth citizen with one parent born in the United Kingdom. Right of abode means that the owner is free from all immigration controls and can move in and out of the United Kingdom without any hindrance although, since 1988, this right has been restricted in the case of a wife in a polygamous marriage. It is more than settlement or indefinite leave to remain (which have some restrictive periods of absence from United Kingdom − see the answers dealing with returning residents − and is indicative of the fact that the holder is not British). See also Chapter 8 under 'Settlement' below (questions 221–223).

Q.18   Does everyone need a sponsor before applying to come to the United Kingdom?

A.   Not in every case. A sponsor is only required where that person is financially responsible for your maintenance and accommodation in United Kingdom. If you can prove that you can satisfy the requirements with your own means, you have a return ticket, enough money to pay for your stay, and are not a child needing parental consent, you do not need a sponsor.

Q.19   Who are considered as 'parents'?

A.   (i) The natural mother and father;

         (ii) the stepfather of a child whose father is dead;

     (iii) the stepmother of a child whose mother is dead;

     (iv) the father and mother of an illegitimate child where the father is proved to be the actual father. An adopted child where the adoption was in accordance with the legal requirements of adoption in the country of adoption and the United Kingdom recognises such foreign adoptive laws (with certain exceptions regarding adoptive parents who settled in the United Kingdom or are being admitted for settlement);

     (v) the person to whom transfer of parental responsibility of a child born in the United Kingdom, where such child is not British, has been given because of the actual parents' inability to look after and care for the child.

Q.20   Who are considered as children for immigration matters?

A.   Children should be under 18 years of age, unmarried, and forming one family unit with the parents. If a child is married or has formed an independent family unit of his own, or is living independently of his/her parents, then such a child will have to apply separately for any entry and will not be accepted to enter under the parents' application in whatever category. As seen above, a stepfather is considered as a parent if the real father of the child is dead and a stepmother will be considered as a parent if the child's mother is dead, and so, conversely, such children will be considered as children of these 'parents'. So, too, will an illegitimate child be considered a child of particular individuals where it is proved that the mother and father are his parents. An adopted child will also be considered the child of the parent applicant if he is adopted according to the rules of the country in which he was adopted, provided the adoption took place before 'a competent administrative authority or a court'. Such countries' adoption orders must be recognised by the United Kingdom (with certain exceptions). In cases where the child is born in the United Kingdom but is not a British citizen, then any genuine transfer of the child to the 'parental control' of someone else due to his actual parent(s)' inability to care for such a child then that person (or persons) will be regarded as a parent or parents. Adoption is a very complex matter and advice should be sought if any such child is to enter with the parents.

Q.21   What if I overstay the period granted me?

A.   You become an 'overstayer' from the moment your leave runs out, unless you have applied for renewal or extension before the period granted to you expires. If you do not obtain such extension you can be detained and removed from the United Kingdom. It is also an offence.

Q.22 What is 'the common travel area' (CTA)?

A. The United Kingdom consists of England, Wales, Scotland, and Northern Ireland. In addition to the United Kingdom, the Republic of Ireland, the Isle of Man, and the Channel Islands, all form the CTA. This means that once someone has entered lawfully through any of these countries, he can travel freely and without any need for permits to the other countries mentioned. Having said that, it does not mean that if you do not require a visa for entry through England then you do not need one for entry through Ireland. Each place has its own list of visa countries and it is advisable to check from each country's mission in the country from which you are coming to see if you are a visa national and to obtain visas to enter. Once entry has been effected then there should be no further problem in travelling within the CTA. (See question 23 below for more on the future of the CTA.)

Q.23 When I enter the common travel area would I need a permit to travel from the country that I entered to any of the other countries in the CTA?

A. The answer is no. You can normally travel to anywhere within the common travel area. However, certain persons who enter through the Republic of Ireland do require leave to enter: those who merely passed through the Republic of Ireland, visa nationals, those who entered the Republic of Ireland unlawfully, those excluded from entry to the United Kingdom on grounds of the public good, those entering the Republic from the United Kingdom and islands after entering unlawfully or overstaying their leave to remain in the United Kingdom will all require leave to enter (see *R v Governor of Ashford Remand Centre ex parte Bougazou* (1983) Imm.A.R. 69). Those who are visa nationals who wish to visit both countries are advised to obtain separate visas in their home countries. Those who are not citizens of the Irish Republic, and only have a visa for the Republic of Ireland, although they do not require leave to enter the United Kingdom, are deemed to have leave to enter for three months with a prohibition on employment (the Immigration (Control of Entry through the Republic of Ireland) order 1972). No stamp will be placed on their passports, however, as there are no immigration controls between the two countries. If such persons wish to remain in the United Kingdom for longer than three months they should apply to the United Kingdom Home Office for an extension of their stay and they should show the date of their arrival in the United Kingdom.

There is a move in European Union countries to standardise entry requirements and free movement within the signatory countries. Recently, the Schenegen Treaty, signed originally by Belgium, France, Germany, Holland, Portugal, Spain and Luxembourg, allows free movement between those countries. Italy and Greece ratified this treaty in 1995. The United Kingdom, however, is not (yet) a signatory. At the moment this move is aimed primarily at free movements of citizens of the EU countries but whether the United Kingdom common travel area will thereby be enlarged to permit anyone outside the EU who has a visa to enter any of those countries within the EU which are signatories, and to be able to travel without further checks, is not quite clear. Until the United Kingdom signs this treaty and it is agreed that anyone with a visa to enter any of the countries mentioned may travel freely in the other countries, the CTA will remain as mentioned in question 22 above and in this answer.

Q.24 **Having entered the United Kingdom lawfully, can I then travel freely to other countries which form the European Union – the United Kingdom being part of the European Union?**

A.   No. Unless you are a citizen of one of the member countries, each country, apart from the CTA mentioned above, will require a visa to allow you to enter. You must apply for information and, where necessary, for a visa either before coming to the United Kingdom or, whilst in the United Kingdom, you must apply at the relevant Embassy or High Commission. If the United Kingdom signs the Schenegen Treaty then you may be able to travel from the United Kingdom to those countries in the EU which are mentioned in question 23 above.

Q.25 **Which countries form the European Union?**

A.   England, Wales, Scotland, Northern Ireland, Republic of Ireland, Belgium, Denmark, France, Germany, Greece, Italy, Luxembourg, the Netherlands, Portugal, Spain, Austria, Sweden, Norway and Finland.

Q.26 **Can any other type of British passport entitle free entry to the United Kingdom?**

A.   Those holding:

(i) British dependent territory passports;

  (ii) British overseas citizens passports;

  (iii) British national (overseas) passports;

  (iv) British protected person passport;

  (v)   British subjects (of a certain category)

can enter the United Kingdom freely provided the passport was issued in the United Kingdom and islands, or in the Republic of Ireland, prior to 1 January 1973 and provided that such a passport does not have the endorsement that the holder is subject to immigration control.

British overseas citizens who hold such United Kingdom passports, wherever they were issued, and can show that they have, since 1 March 1968, been given indefinite leave to enter or remain in United Kingdom may be given indefinite leave to enter.

Q.27 What are the immigration rules?

A.   These are rules made and passed in the House of Commons and are published by the Home Office. They show how immigration officers should act *vis-à-vis* the Immigration Act 1971. They explain the requirements for each type of entry, for settlement, and so forth. They are to be complied with by both the intending entrant (or those who have already entered) and by the immigration officials. Anyone not satisfied with the interpretation of the rules by an immigration officer who refuses him entry can appeal to an adjudicator. The present rules – HC395 – are derived from various previous sets of rules and have been consolidated into one set of rules that came into effect on 1 October 1994.

All applications must be made for certain categories of entry specified within the rules as published. There are also 'rules outside the rules' (my own description). By this I mean that the Home Office may consider applications outside the rules (as published) and may use discretion in deciding those applications. If this results in a refusal there is no right of appeal. From time to time, however, the Home Office gives directives to entry clearance officers and immigration officers as to how to deal with certain situations not covered by the published rules.

There are also certain rules that apply if an application is made outside the rules (concerning 'compassionate grounds', for example). These rules are not published for the general public but are policies laid down for immigration purposes. In certain circumstances they become so well established that they become the norm. Where this is the case, failure to follow such policies without giving reasons for doing so has been ruled to be unfair and perverse (*R v SSHD ex parte Benjamin Amankwah* (1994) Imm.A.R. 240).

Q.28 **Apart from the rules what other legislation, orders or rules are there relating to immigration?**

A. The 1971 Immigration Act is the main Act and the British Nationality Act 1981 (which came into effect in 1983) is also quite relevant. Certain portions of these Acts have been amended by the Immigration Act 1988. Other Acts and regulations relating to Immigration are the following:

Immigration (Control of Entry Through The Republic of Ireland) order 1972

Immigration (Exemption from Control) order 1972

Immigration (Revocation of Employment Restrictions) order 1972

Immigration (Particulars of Passengers and Crew) order 1972

Immigration (Hotel Records) order 1972

Immigration (Registration with Police) regulations 1972

Immigration (Pakistan Act) 1973 – Channel Islands and Isle of Man order 1973

Immigration (Landing and Embarkation Cards) order 1975

Immigration (Variation of Leave) order 1976, amended 1989

Immigration Appeals (Procedure) rules 1984

Immigration (Notices) regulations 1984

Hong Kong (British Nationality) order 1986

Immigration (Ports of Entry) order 1987

Immigration Act 1988

British Nationality (Hong Kong) Act 1990

British Nationality (Hong Kong – Registration of Citizens) regulations 1990

The Channel-Tunnel (Fire Services, Immigration and Prevention of Terrorism) order 1990

British Nationality (Hong Kong)(Selection Scheme) order 1990

Immigration Carriers' Liability (Prescribed Sum) order 1991

Immigration (Isle of Man) order 1991

Asylum and Immigration Appeals Act 1993

Immigration (Restricted Rights of Appeal Against Deportation) (exemption order) 1993

Immigration (transit visa) order 1993;

Immigration (Guernsey) order 1993;

Immigration (Jersey) order 1993;

Immigration and Appeals (Procedure) rules 1993;

Command paper 2663 – 1994;

The UNHCR Convention 1951 and Protocol 1967 (the UNHCR Handbook) are of direct relevance to immigration (asylum).

The Diplomatic Privileges Act 1964 is also relevant.

The Social Security (Persons from Abroad) Miscellaneous Amendments Regulations 1996.

Housing Bill and the Asylum and Immigration Bill will become relevant if passed in due course later in 1996.

The Immigration Appeals Reports, commonly referred to by practitioners as the Green Book, contain reports of cases.

Q.29 **To whom does an applicant who has been refused entry or other applications appeal?**

A. The immigration appeals system is distinct from the general courts of law up to a point. In the first instance an adjudicator hears your appeal and then it may move higher to the Immigration Appeals Tribunal. In some cases it may go for judicial review in a court.

Q.30   Who are adjudicators?

A.   They are appointed by the Lord Chancellor's office to hear cases involving immigration matters and they sit alone. They need not be lawyers. 'Special adjudicators' who deal with asylum cases. They hear appeals in special places such as Thanet House in Fleet Street, London. These are not 'law courts' as generally understood.

Q.31   What is the Tribunal?

A.   An appeal from the adjudicator lies with the Immigration Appeals Tribunal. Three people make up the panel and the chairman is usually a barrister. They deal with appeals from the adjudicators. Their decisions or dicta will be binding on the adjudicators in the same way that an ordinary Appeal Court's decision is binding on the High Court or other lower courts. Leave to appeal to the Tribunal must be obtained before the appeal can go to the Tribunal. From 1993, appeals from the Tribunal must be made to the Court of Appeal with prior leave (Asylum and Immigration Appeals Act 1993).

Q.32   What is judicial review?

A.   This is where the normal court of law comes in. A judicial review is made under the High Court rules (Ord 53 r3). Leave must first be obtained and there is a special form for immigration matters. Leave may be obtained on limited grounds – illegality, irrationality, or procedural impropriety – and application for leave must first be made by a barrister. If this is made to the Tribunal, the matter proceeds before a judge for review. If leave is refused then further proceedings may follow in the Court of Appeal. If leave is granted, and the hearing is dismissed on appeal by the Tribunal, the appellant can apply to the Tribunal for leave to take the matter to the Court of Appeal. Leave to go for judicial review is usually difficult to obtain and judicial review challenges mostly concern deportation on grounds of illegal entry.

Q.33   Are there time limits for an appeal to be brought?

A.   Yes. It is essential that appeals are brought within the time limits set down for each appeal. Some appeals have shorter time limits than others – particularly certain asylum appeals which allow as little as two days for notice of appeal to be lodged. It is advisable for the applicant to decide from the inception of any application whether an appeal will be lodged if it is refused and to be ready to appeal immediately if an adverse decision is given (see Chapter 11).

Q34. **If leave to enter is refused can a person get temporary admission (TA)?**

A. Temporary admission is an alternative to detention. When someone arrives at a port or airport with a view to gaining entry to the United Kingdom the immigration officer considers whether to grant him entry or not depending on whether he satisfies the requirements for the category under which he is seeking entry. If the decision is not made immediately, the person concerned may either be detained at one of the detention centres or he can apply for temporary admission. He can apply even whilst detained. If permission is granted it means that he will give an address where he will stay until a decision to grant or refuse him entry is made. He can move freely but may have to report to the police or immigration officer daily or as directed. If the applicant is refused entry he will then be removed from the United Kingdom. Temporary admission is not leave to enter or remain.

Temporary admission is relevant to illegal entrants awaiting removal and to asylum-seekers awaiting a decision on their applications. There is no right of appeal except where the entrant arrived with an entry clearance or visa; here TA may be given for the purpose of an appeal against refusal of entry. Normally where TA is granted the passport will be held by the immigration authorities until the date required for the applicant to report to them.

Where TA is refused, reasons must be given for such refusal together with the grounds on which the refusal is based (for example, that the applicant will disappear). A general statement that the applicant will not comply with all or any of the conditions for granting TA is not sufficient. All refusals must be explained to the applicant in language that he understands and must be recorded and justified by an immigration inspector when he reviews the decision to refuse (HO instructions, 1994). It is always advisable for an applicant to consult an adviser and to have one accompany him. He may be able to find out why only TA was given, or why it was refused, and to have the matter redressed if possible.

Q.35 **What is variation of leave and curtailment?**

A. This is where the person who wishes to enter or has entered into the

United Kingdom in one category (for example as a visitor) wishes to change to another category (such as a holidaymaker) or where he wishes to have the period of leave granted extended. He can apply initially by letter to the Under Secretary of State at Lunar House if he is in the United Kingdom, stating in simple terms what the application is for. This should be sufficient until the fuller grounds, documents and evidence are forwarded (shortly afterwards) (*Re Brown* (1976) Imm.A.R. 119). This simple application, signed by the applicant himself, is useful where time is very short and enables the applicant to make the application within the period of his limited leave.

The new rules state that such variations will be refused if the variation is for a purpose not covered by the rules, and appeals against such refusals will not be allowed. If the person concerned ceases to meet the requirements of the rules pertaining to his category of entry he will be refused entry or variation of his leave or his leave may be curtailed.

Other grounds for refusal of variation of leave (as has been mentioned in an earlier answer) are: making a false representation or failure to disclose material facts so as to obtain entry or variation*; failure to comply with any of the requirements for entry or to remain in any category*; failure of the applicant to maintain or accommodate himself and dependants according to the rules*; being a threat to national security*; character, conduct, and association*; refusal by sponsor to give a written undertaking when so requested as to accommodation and maintenance, or failure to honour such undertaking; failure to honour any declaration or undertaking as to intended length of stay or purpose of visit; inability to satisfy the immigration officer that the applicant will return to another country if he is allowed to remain for a further period (this is not required where the person qualifies for settlement or is the spouse of such a person); failure of the applicant to produce documents or other evidence to support his claim to remain under the rules, or even to produce such documents or evidence within a reasonable time; failure to attend an interview without reasonable excuse; failure of someone under 18 years of age to provide his parents' consent (if required) if the application is not made by the parents, except in the case of a child seeking asylum.

When application is made for variation of leave in time, and it is refused, the applicant will be given 28 days extension from the date of the decision by the Home Office. A right of appeal against refusal of the variation exists and the applicant can stay until the appeal processes are exhausted.

In some cases, leave to remain will be cut short. This is known as 'curtailment'. These instances are marked with an asterisk (*) in the previous paragraph. The Home Office has the power to curtail any leave granted under the rules for good reasons. Where leave is granted outside the rules (for example, on concessions – see the section of this book dealing with concessions) then it has no power under those rules to curtail on the grounds that the person no longer meets the requirements of the rules. It can, however, curtail under the Immigration Act 1971 s3(3)(a) (*In re Funtanares* no. 9040, *R v IAT* (1992), *In re Shukla* (1992) case no. 9023).

Q.36 **Do Commonwealth citizens have to register with the police in the United Kingdom? How is registration carried out?**

A. Where there is a condition requiring registration with the police, this will be shown on the passport. The person concerned takes his passport with two passport-size photographs to the police and a fee is payable and this is fairly high. The following are normally required to do this as mentioned earlier:

    (i) any foreign national aged 16 or over given limited leave for longer than three months if he is in permit-free employment as a domestic servant in a diplomatic household, or as a minister of religion.

    (ii) any foreign national aged 16 or over given leave to enter for longer than six months if such person is:

        (a) a student;

        (b) an au pair;

        (c) a businessman or self-employed;

        (d) an investor;

        (e) a person of independent means;

        (f) an artist;

        (g) a spouse or child of someone required to register;

        (h) a family member of a national of the European Economic Area who is himself not a national of the European Economic Area countries (see Immigration (European Economic Area) order 1994);

        (i) in some cases where there was no requirement to register on entry such registration may be imposed.

Commonwealth citizens are not normally required to register.

Q.37   What is meant by 'public funds'?

A.   Public funds have been defined by the rules as income support, family credit, council tax benefits, housing benefits (under part 7 of the Social Security Contributions and Benefits Act 1992 and also under a similar Act for Northern Ireland (1992)), and housing (under Part 3 of the Housing Act 1985, Part 2 of the Housing (Northern Ireland) order 1988, and Part 2 of the Housing (Scotland) Act 1987. These funds are provided by the State to help British citizens, and certain people who are in the United Kingdom such as those who have settled here, those granted refugees status, those with exceptional leave to remain, asylum-seekers, and work permit holders, and are not intended for people who come in as visitors and certain other categories on limited leave to remain.

Where there is a sponsor, public funds will include capital saved by the sponsor out of supplementary benefits (*R v IAT ex parte Chhinderpal Singh* (1989) Imm.A.R. 69). However, a less strict practice applies where there are other residents in a household, apart from the sponsor, receiving public funds, and this should not affect the sponsor. It is only where additional recourse to public funds would be necessary on the applicant's arrival that this could cause a problem. The sponsor's means, including any public funds to which he is entitled in his own right, must be sufficient to provide adequate maintenance and accommodation for the applicant and dependant(s), if any. Where a visitor has need to fall back on help by the United Kingdom government for his maintenance and accommodation through no fault of his own, he may receive limited help for a short period but any extension of his application to stay will not be granted and he stands the chance of having his leave curtailed and may damage his chances if he seeks to remain permanently. Another great disadvantage is the possibility of being refused entry into the United Kingdom in future. See the postscript for new restrictions that came into force in 1996.

Q.38   What is meant by 'adequate accommodation' and 'exclusive accommodation'?

A.   In some cases the rules require adequate accommodation. This means accommodation that will hold the number of persons coming to live there. A one-bedroom flat will suffice for a man and wife, perhaps with a young baby, but if there are children who will need separate beds then it will be advisable to be able to accommodate boys separately from girls, and to accommodate at most two or three children of the same sex to a room, depending on their ages.

In some cases, where a person is coming alone, accommodation is required to be adequate but not necessarily 'exclusive'. When he is being joined by his spouse (and children) some categories call for exclusive accommodation. This means that the accommodation (including bathroom/toilets/kitchen) must not be shared by other persons not making up the family unit. This exclusivity requirement has been relaxed (see question 225(e)). The accommodation must be either owned or rented.

Q.39 What is meant by maintenance?

A. This is the amount of money left for use by the entrant or his sponsor after deducting all overhead expenses like rent, lighting, water, and gas bills. The remaining amount should be enough to support him and his dependants during the period of his stay. An adequate sum may be £100 – 120 a week depending on the season and the area. London may be more expensive.

Q.40 What is a 'prohibition on' or a 'restriction from' employment?

A. When the passport is stamped with the following: 'Leave to enter the United Kingdom on condition that the holder does not enter employment paid or unpaid and does not engage in any business or profession, is hereby given until ... ' it is a 'prohibition'.

Where the passport is stamped with the following: 'Leave to enter the United Kingdom, on condition that the holder does not enter or change employment paid or unpaid without the consent of the Secretary of State for Employment, and does not engage in any business or profession without the consent of the Secretary of State for Home Department, is hereby given until ... ' it is a 'restriction'.

The rules normally call for a prohibition on employment unless the period granted to the entrant is twelve months or longer. The stamp for a restriction speaks for itself – permission must be obtained before taking up employment.

Q.41 What is meant by 'close connections' with the United Kingdom?

A. This is decided upon on the facts of each case and is to be considered in the context of relationships elsewhere than in the United Kingdom to see whether the applicant has closer links with people in the United Kingdom than with those outside. For this purpose, in immigration, there is no distinction between blood relationships and those by affinity (people such as daughters-in-law). The existence of an eldest son in the United Kingdom who is a British citizen may suffice as evidence of a close connection with the United Kingdom, even if there are other sons or daughters elsewhere, if, for example, it can be shown that the eldest son is, by custom, the one who is looked upon as closest in line and responsibility. Ownership of property in the United Kingdom and long periods of residence may show close connections. (See *Yuen-on Fung, Wai-yin Fung v ECO Hong Kong* (1984) Imm.A.R. 159). In one case (*re Sum Yee Thong* (TH/30896/87)) it was held that, in a 'gay relationship', a partner in the United Kingdom was helpful in establishing a close relationship by the applicant seeking entry as a person of independent means but, by contrast, having friends in the United Kingdom is not sufficient.

In Chapter 1 I have tried to give a basic understanding of the terms and phrases commonly used. In the following parts the questions and answers will deal with specific categories of entrants.

Chapter 2

Visitors

ORDINARY VISITS

Q.42   How long can a visitor be allowed to stay in the United Kingdom?

A.   Six months is the maximum. He may apply for less but not more. If he applies for more than six months the application will be refused outright, the refusal will be noted on the passport, and it will be more difficult to obtain entry next time as the immigration authorities will be suspicious of the applicant's intention to return. If the application is for less than six months the visitor can apply for an extension whilst in the United Kingdom to make up the six months, but he will have to do so before the expiry of the period granted and he will have to show that he can satisfy all the requirements for his stay for the rest of the extended period.

Q.43   Do all arrivals need entry clearance?

A.   No. British citizens and those with a right of abode do not need it as they can come and go as they please, as can BOCs with settlement status for the time being. Visitors from visa countries must get visas or entry clearances. Other citizens may, if they so wish, obtain these and if they do they will find it easier to enter the United Kingdom and will have a right of appeal if they are refused. Each entry clearance is valid for one visit only and cannot be used for a second visit, even when the period granted has not expired. In some cases multiple entry clearances can be applied for – this would apply to businessmen or other visitors who make frequent short visits to the United Kingdom – and these are valid for two years. (See also answers to questions 6–9. Transit visitors should see the section on visitors in transit below.)

Q.44   If a visit is sponsored, who makes the application for entry clearance?

A.   If he is from a non-visa country but wishes to obtain prior entry clearance, the visitor should go to the Embassy or High Commission in his own country and apply himself. He will produce the sponsor's letter of invitation and other necessary evidence to show that accommodation is available and the source of income from which the visitor will be maintained. If he does not wish to do so then the procedure is the same when he confronts the immigration officer in the United Kingdom. Visa nationals need an entry visa from their home country but the requirements are the same as for non-visa nationals.

Q.45   What are the requirements for a visit?

A.   The new rules state that the intending visitor must satisfy the ECO (entry clearance officer) if he is getting his clearance or visa abroad or the IO (immigration officer on arrival in the United Kingdom – if he is not a visa national) on the following points:

> (i) that he can maintain himself and dependants travelling with him adequately without recourse to 'public funds' and without working;

> (ii) that he can accommodate himself and any dependants travelling with him without recourse to public funds and without working;

> (iii) that he can meet the cost of his return fare. He will invariably be required to show a return ticket and it is much easier if he has one when he applies;

> (iv) that he intends to return to his country at the end of the visit. Great emphasis is placed on an 'intention test' (see questions 48 and 49 below);

> (v) that the intention is a genuine visit for a period not exceeding six months;

> (vi) that during his visit he will not take up employment;

> (vii) that he does not intend to take up studies at a maintained school;

> (viii) that he does not intend to produce any goods or services for sale to the public.

Q.46   Apart from the above, will I have to show a reason for visiting?

A.   One of the first things you will be asked will certainly be the reason for your visit. You are advised to give a truthful answer (for example, to spend some time with your relatives, or to have private medical care, or to look into the possibilities of studying later on when you have gone back and assessed the possibilities, to see another part of the world before settling down abroad to work or to have a family, or whatever other reasons you may have). A visit 'to better oneself' has been rejected. A visit to enable a relative to go out to work has been disapproved whilst, in another case, a visit to help a relative in some temporary matter has not been rejected. Each case will be assessed on its own merits. Wealth is also a vital consideration. A wealthy visitor who wishes to visit the zoo or to see the Tower of London will find his application less difficult than someone who had to scrape and save for a long time for such a visit.

Some sportsmen or entertainers are allowed to enter as visitors if they are coming for an audition and for personal appearances which do not entail a performance. (See the relevant section for more on this.)

Q.47 **With regard to accommodation and maintenance, will the visitor have to show that he can provide both by himself?**

A. No. If he and his dependants were invited to come over then his sponsor will have to provide a letter to that effect and show that he can maintain and accommodate himself (and them) without having to call for help from public funds (see above, questions 37–39) and without the visitor having to go out to work. Where visitors are sponsored it is advisable for the sponsor to meet them at the airport or port and bring evidence of the financial support available to them (bank statements, wage slips, savings) and also evidence of the accommodation available (see above). If the sponsor cannot come to meet the visitor he must have a contact telephone number which the visitor can give to the officer to make immediate contact with the sponsor. If he is not sponsored, then travellers' cheques for a sum adequate to cover all his expenses will have to be shown as well as evidence of arrangements made for accommodation (see question 18 above).

Q.48 **What form does the 'intention to return' test take?**

A. This test is to show that you are a genuine visitor and not one who will try to stay in the United Kingdom after the period granted expires. The ECO or IO will take great pains to investigate this and you will be questioned in detail about your background, work, schooling (if you are of school age), care of children and family left behind, the money you have to spend and what happens when it runs out. Will you find employment? Will you take up a course of studies if you find a suitable one? They will question you at length to prove your actual intention of going back or staying. Luggage may be examined at the port of entry and letters may be read to discover your intention. Any doubt by the ECO or IO of your intention to return will result in difficulty in entering. Lack of incentive to return to your country, although not necessarily in itself a reason for refusing, can be taken into account. Previous visits when you returned to your country within the period granted should be taken into account (see also question 76 below).

Q.49   What do I have to do to show that I intend to return?

A.   Any convincing proof that you will have to return will be vital. Examples might include having all your friends in your country, the climate in the United Kingdom being warm for the period of the visit (particularly if the visit is during summer here and will last until near winter time), a business abroad, employment abroad (a letter from an employer granting leave for short period of your visit would be useful here), if attending school or college proof that the visit is being made during a vacation and evidence that you will be continuing at school (evidence of payment of fees will be useful), any social standing you have abroad, home and property owned – these may all be helpful. If you are employed, your salary will be taken into account and the reason for high expenses for such a short visit may be questioned unless the visit is sponsored. People from poor countries, people with several relatives in United Kingdom, younger people, elderly people, unemployed people, or students who have just finished their courses are all under greater suspicion than others. Mere suspicion, however, is not sufficient for the ECO or IO to refuse entry clearance or entry.

Q.50   Can a visitor transact business during his visit?

A.   Yes. He can make contacts with business firms, investigate new products, or even learn new techniques, make purchases of products for sale abroad, attend trade fairs or seminars and classroom training, and can sign or enter into contracts. He cannot set up a business or a branch of his business abroad nor can he seek employment whether paid or unpaid. His visit must not result in his doing 'productive work' such as preparing a report or collecting and analysing data and making reports to a United Kingdom company. He may not produce goods or provide services within the United Kingdom, including the selling of goods or services direct to members of the public.

        Application for 'business visitor's' clearance can be more complicated than it seems and only a general guideline has been given in this answer. Anyone coming to the United Kingdom as a business visitor and who is not too certain as to whether his application should be for a mere visit or whether what he is coming to do may need a work permit should seek further advice.

Q.51 Can a visitor apply to extend his stay?

A.   As stated in the answer to question 42 above, the maximum period allowed by the rules is six months and, where a period less than that was originally applied for, application can be made for an extension. An explanation for the change of plan must be acceptable as must proof that the visitor can satisfy the other requirements for staying (see question 45).

If the visitor had six months granted and wished to stay beyond this period there is nothing stopping him from applying before the expiry date of his leave but this will be outside the rules and can only be at the discretion of the Home Office – and such applications are only granted in exceptional circumstances. Changes in the rules state that those admitted for six months will not be permitted to extend their visits. Refusals will result in the passport being marked accordingly and this will make it very difficult for the visitor to obtain entry to the United Kingdom in future and may even put him at risk of not being able to obtain entry into other countries. If the reason is important then any such application should state the precise reason, its importance, the exact period requested, and any evidence that the visitor intends to return to his own country. The application may be made by letter and it is usual to send one's passport at the same time. The visitor can request his passport at any time and, if it is required for travelling, the application for extension will be deemed to be withdrawn.

Q.52 What are the conditions or requirements for a permanent stay if a visitor gets married?

A.   A visitor can get married but if he wishes to stay in the United Kingdom permanently then he must satisfy the following conditions:

   (a) the other spouse must be a British citizen or one who has settlement status;

   (b) the main intention (primary purpose) of the marriage must not be to obtain settlement status;

   (c) the parties to the marriage must have met each other;

(d) both parties must live together as husband and wife and the relationship must be permanent;

(e) the visitor getting married must not have breached the immigration rules;

(f) the marriage must not have taken place after a decision to deport the visitor has been made, or after he has been recommended for deportation by a court, or after a deportation order has actually been made;

(g) the marriage must still exist at the time of the application to stay in the United Kingdom permanently (it will be pointless to apply for settlement if before the six month visit period is up the visitor has married and then divorced);

(h) both spouses must have adequate accommodation without recourse to 'public funds' (see questions 37–39);

(i) they must be able to maintain themselves and any dependants adequately and without recourse to 'public funds' (see questions 37–39).

Points (a), (b) and (c) above are meant to deal with what is commonly referred to as a 'marriage of convenience' or 'immigration marriage'. It has been known for some marriages to be arranged with British citizens for the purpose of obtaining settlement; afterwards each party goes his/her own way. These arrangements are very expensive and are illegal for the purpose of immigration. A visitor must be very wary of any such arrangement and avoid it altogether. Someone who is here on a six months visiting visa will create a great deal of suspicion if he applies during his stay for indefinite leave to remain on the grounds of marriage. The visitor will then have to satisfy the Secretary of State for Home Affairs (Home Office) about all the conditions above. Each of the conditions has criteria which are used to decide whether the condition has been met. These will be dealt with in the appropriate sections below.

If the Secretary of State is satisfied, the visitor will be granted one year's leave to remain and before that year is up he should then apply for indefinite leave to remain.

Q.53   Generally, can a visitor change his status during his visit?

A.   In certain cases he can if he marries and wishes to stay with his spouse (we have already dealt with this above) or if he applies for settlement to stay with a close relative, or wishes to change from a visitor to a student, or applies for asylum. A visitor who is not a visa national can apply to stay as a student. A visitor who is a visa national will have to leave the United Kingdom before he can apply to become a student. Each of these various applications for change or variation has certain requirements that must be satisfied before it can be granted. A visitor cannot apply to stay to work or to be self-employed, nor would it now appear, under the new rules, that he can change to a working holidaymaker or to go into the work permit training or work experience schemes as it is now required that prior entry clearance or a visa is required to enter for each category. In effect it seems that an application will not be likely to succeed if the change is to a category that needed prior entry clearance or a visa. Each change has its own conditions and requirements that must be satisfied and each will be dealt with under its category.

Q.54   What happens if a visitor arrives without an entry clearance and is held at the airport until a decision is taken to admit him or refuse him entry?

A.   There is no right of appeal whilst the visitor is still in the United Kingdom. He can apply for temporary admission (see question 34) and then seek advice from practitioners or immigration advisers. If a decision as to whether to admit or refuse entry has not yet been given it may be possible to convince the IO to give a favourable decision. Once a refusal has been decided it will be difficult to have this reversed unless the IO can be shown compelling and exceptional grounds or the visitor can prove to the IO that he can make good his initial failure to substantiate his claim for entry.

Q.55   Apart from ordinary visits are any other 'types' of visit permitted?

A.   Yes. A person can come in as a visitor for medical reasons or as a visiting academic or as a type of 'sole representative'. These are all dealt with below. There is also a new category for visitors in transit for up to 48 hours.

MEDICAL VISITS

Q.56   What is the position if a visit is for the purpose of medical treatment?

A.   You may be admitted on coming for private medical treatment if:

(a) the medical inspector at the port of entry is satisfied that you pose no threat to public health if the disease is communicable;

(b) you will return to your country at the end of your treatment;

(c) the treatment is of a finite duration;

(d) you must produce evidence of:

(i) the nature and medical condition of the illness;

(ii) satisfactory arrangement for consultations and necessary treatment by your own doctors;

(iii) the estimated costs of treatment and medication and your ability and undertaking to pay such costs;

(iv) how long the treatment is likely to last.

In addition to the above requirements, the person concerned should be able to satisfy the immigration officer or the entry clearance officer that he can meet all the normal requirements for an ordinary visit as shown in the answers to questions 45 and 46 above. (See *Jacques Foon v SSHD* (1983) Imm.A.R. 29.)

Q.57   If visiting the United Kingdom for medical treatment will six months be the maximum period that will be granted?

A.   The six month period, which is the maximum allowed for an ordinary visitor, is not strictly applicable in this case. An initial period will be given and this can be extended on request and on proof that medical care is still going on. The application must be made before the expiry of the initial period.

It is not a requirement that the treatment needed is not available in the applicant's own country. If it becomes obvious that the applicant's condition or ailment is only minor he may be asked to submit to a medical enquiry before any extension is granted. This is to make sure that he is not merely prolonging his leave unnecessarily. The new rules require that for such an extension to be granted the applicant must continue to meet the requirements of a visitor as set out in the answer to question 45 above as well as those shown in the answer to question 51. In addition he must produce evidence from a 'registered medical practitioner who holds an NHS (National Health Service) consultant post of satisfactory arrangements for private medical consultation or treatment, and its likely duration'. (This particular requirement seems odd in the face of the fact that all such treatment should be private.) Where treatment is in progress at the time of the application for the extension he must be able to prove that he has met all the costs and expenses in the UK and that he has sufficient money in the United Kingdom to pay all such further likely costs and intends to meet such costs. Where all these requirements are met, the Secretary of State may grant a stay or further stay subject to a prohibition of employment.

Q.58   What if the visit is for a medical check-up or assessment?

A.   Leave to enter for medical treatment is not the same as that for check-ups or assessments or any other acts not amounting to actual treatment. Leave as a visitor may be granted, not exceeding six months, for any such visits.

Q.59   What if the treatment is on-going for life?

A.   In such cases where treatment is shown to be lifelong, or where there is no reasonably predictable period for the treatment to end, the Home Office is not likely to extend the period except on exceptionally compassionate grounds.

Q.60   If the treatment needs visits at widely spaced intervals will a continuous stay between treatments be granted?

A.   The answer is normally no.

ACADEMIC VISITS

Q.61   What are the requirements for an academic visit?

A.   The requirements for a work permit for such visits may be waived in certain cases where the visits are for short periods. Those sponsored by educational-orientated charities or research organisation may be given leave to enter if the visitor does not receive payment in the United Kingdom by United Kingdom funders. Payment does not include funding the visitor's expenses. A permit is also conditional upon the visitor not taking up appointment to a post which can be filled by United Kingdom (or European Union) residents. The visit must also be in preparation for a career abroad and may not exceed 12 months.

Q.62   What is the period granted for an academic visit?

A.   The initial period will be for up to six months (the maximum period granted to an ordinary visitor) but this period may be extended on application to 12 months. Entry clearance must be obtained abroad where the person is a visa-national but it may be advantageous to obtain entry clearance where he is not, in that the visitor may be admitted for 12 months at the port of entry.

Q.63   What if the academic visitor does not meet the requirements set out above?

A.   He will need a work permit and will also need a work permit if, from the outset, his visit will last more than 12 months.

VISITORS IN TRANSIT

Q.64   What are the requirements for a visitor in transit?

A.   If the visitor is not a member of a ship's, aircraft's, hovercraft's, hydrofoil's, or train's crew, and is seeking entry as a visitor in transit, he will be granted not more than 48 hours' stay and then he will have to transit to another country. Before leave is given for such a short visit he must also show that he has the means and intention to travel to the other country, that such other country is not within the common travel area (see answers to questions 22 and 23) and that he is assured of entry there (that is, if a visa or entry clearance is needed by him to enter that country he must have it), and that he can and intends to leave the United Kingdom within 48 hours. Where no airline will carry him to his destination he will be deemed not to have the means of proceeding to that other country (*R v SSHD ex parte Connye* (1987) Imm.A.R. 478). He will be prohibited from employment.

The new rules are unclear as to what happens where, due to a strike or delay resulting from bad weather or any other reason, a passenger is forced to remain longer than 48 hours and is forced, without any fault on his part, to become an overstayer. Any application by a visitor-in-transit for an extension of stay beyond the 48 hours will be refused. Perhaps in a case of compassionate circumstances the Home Office might consider an extension but this will be outside the rules.

Certain transit passengers will not need visas. The transit without visa concession will apply to such persons. They will not need a visa if they are booked on an onward flight within 24 hours of their arrival and have all the necessary visas and documentation for onward travel to their destination. A list of such passengers from certain countries is in existence and is revised every so often – in 1995 Chinese, Nigerians and Ghanaians were placed on the list of those requiring transit visas. Lebanese passengers were taken off the list.

VISITS BY ENTERTAINERS / FILM CREWS

Q.65 **What are the rules relating to entertainers or film crews visiting the United Kingdom?**

A.   The general position is that they need entry clearances to come in and need a work permit to come and work here. If they are employed to come and perform in the United Kingdom they should have a work permit and the employer applies for this. There are several requirements to be satisfied before the Department of Employment will issue a work permit. Footballers have an additional form to fill in for a work permit.

Those coming for short visits for one or more performances may be admitted without a work permit, provided they are amateurs. This is a concession outside the rules. They must not be coming to establish themselves here nor must they be a threat to local labour in this field. Such visits will be for not more than six months. In this category are solo performers, members of a group such as a choir group, youth orchestras, and school dramatic groups coming for one or more specifically arranged engagements. It will not matter if they are coming with the aim of making money (for example fund-raising for their group or for charities) as long as they are amateurs. Where professionals are coming to take part in shows for charity they will be allowed in as long as they are not earning fees or their group is not coming for profit. Those coming as professional entertainers in order to take part in inter-cultural shows sponsored by the respective governments, or by international organisations, or professional musicians taking part in music competitions will also be allowed entry outside the rules for such visits.

Where the entertainer is coming to transact business such as signing contracts or for promotional purposes (such as appearing in a chat show on radio or television) he may be allowed in as a business visitor but, as has been mentioned above, he must not earn fees. Entertainers coming in as visitors or under a category that does not require a work permit may be allowed in without an entry clearance if they are not visa nationals, otherwise an entry clearance or visa will be required as is normally the case. It is advisable for such a person, who is coming as a visitor but to entertain, to have a letter from his organisation confirming the purpose of the visit. It may be helpful for such a person to obtain an entry clearance before even leaving his country if he is not a visa national.

Film crews may be admitted without a work permit for six months if coming as visitors but will use their time (six months maximum granted to visitors) to film location sequences.

Chapter 3

Professional workers

DOCTORS, DENTISTS, LAWYERS

Q.66 **What are the requirements for doctors and dentists seeking entry for postgraduate training?**

A. In order for a doctor or dentist to enter the United Kingdom for post-graduate training the doctor or dentist:

(1)(i) must be a graduate from a medical school in the United Kingdom with the intention of taking pre-registration house officer employment for up to 12 months. This is a General Medical Council requirement for doctors and dentists in order to get full regististration with the Council, and

(ii) the applicant must not have spent more than the 12 months in total in the pre-registration house officer employment;

or

(2)(i) he must be eligible for full or limited registration with the Council (medical or dental) and must intend to undertake postgraduate training in a hospital, and

(ii) he must not have not spent more than four years in aggregate in Britain as a postgraduate doctor or dentist. This period does not include any pre-registration house officer employment.

Q.67 **How long will a doctor or dentist be given to stay?**

A. The initial period will be 12 months.

Q.68 **Can this period be extended?**

A. Yes. If he meets the alternative requirements mentioned in question 66 (1)(i) above and would not as a result of such extension spend more than 12 months in total (to be aggregated) in employment as a pre-registration house officer or if he meets the requirement of (2)(i) mentioned in question 66 above and would not, as a result of such extension, spend more than four years in total (to be aggregated) in the United Kingdom as a postgraduate doctor or dentist (such period does not include the 12 months spent in pre-registration house officer employment) and he intends to leave the United Kingdom at the end of his training period, then his extension can be granted for a period of 12 months.

Q.69   Does a doctor or dentist need prior entry clearance?

A.   If he is from a visa country then yes. If he is not then the ordinary rules for visiting apply. Remember, however, that if no prior entry clearance has been obtained for this purpose, and he is refused entry, there is no appeal within the United Kingdom against the decision. It is advisable to obtain a visa.

Q.70   Will the spouse be allowed in?

A.   The new rules do not seem to distinguish greatly between students and doctors/dentists doing postgraduate training. The requirements for a spouse to enter are therefore: that the doctor's/dentist's spouse should be a genuine spouse – that they should be married and should intend to live with each other during their stay; that the marriage should subsist for the period to be granted; that they should have adequate accommodation and maintenance for themselves and any dependants without recourse to public funds (mentioned previously); that the incoming spouse should not intend to take up employment (except where such leave to enter or remain is for 12 months or more), and that the applicant should intend to leave the United Kingdom at the end of the period granted him/her.

Q.71   Will the children be allowed in?

A.   If the children are under 18, are not married, and have not formed any independent family units (in other words, are not married but are living with someone independently of the parents, or even just living independently on their own without the parents' support), can be accommodated and maintained adequately without recourse to public funds, and will return to their country at the end of the period granted them, they will be given leave to enter/remain. Their eligibility to work is the same as for a spouse mentioned above.

Q.72. What of lawyers wishing to come to the United Kingdom to practise?

A. The Home Office has stated to Butterworths that solicitors, barristers and consultants in overseas law coming to work here in the United Kingdom generally do not need to invest the £200 000 that is required of other overseas businessmen or self-employed persons. Those coming to set themselves up in practice, or to join an existing practice as a partner, are admitted on a concessionary basis outside the immigration rules. Applicants must first obtain entry clearance abroad before travelling. In some cases the Home Office may waive the entry clearance requirement and consider an application made from within the United Kingdom. They must be able to satisfy the entry clearance officer that they are able to maintain and accommodate themselves and any dependants without taking other work or having recourse to public funds.

Barristers and solicitors are required to provide evidence from the appropriate Law Society, Bar Council or Chambers of their eligibility to practise in this country.

Barristers wishing to practise from home must also have Bar Council permission to do so. Consultants in overseas laws are required to provide evidence of their qualifications and a letter from the appropriate Law Society confirming that there is no objection to the application being granted. Those overseas lawyers who intend to establish a new practice here must additionally show that they have the financial resources to do so.

Barristers must have been called to the Bar in the United Kingdom, must have been offered a tenancy in Chambers, must have sufficient funds to meet their share of chambers' expenses, and must be of good character.

Barristers/solicitors who practise in a fused profession based on qualifications obtained in the United Kingdom are advised, in addition to the above requirements, to obtain a letter from the Chambers or solicitor's firm confirming that they have been accepted as members of Chambers or of the firm.

Those who qualified in the United Kingdom but have not qualified as practitioners in the United Kingdom will now have to do a vocational course and pupillage and the cost is about £3800.

Chapter 4

Students

Q.73 **Does a student need an entry clearance or a visa before coming to the United Kingdom to study?**

A. A non-visa national does not need an entry clearance but it is safer to obtain one as the bearer is much less likely to be refused entry at the port or airport and would also have a right of appeal if he is refused entry having obtained an entry clearance. Visa nationals need a visa before coming.

Q.74 **What are the requirements that a student must satisfy before he will be granted an entry clearance or visa or be allowed into Britain?**

A. He must satisfy the ECO or visa officer or IO

   (1) that he has been accepted for a course of study at:

      (a) a publicly funded institution of further or higher education (such as a university or a polytechnic), or

      (b) an independent fee-paying school, that is not within the maintained sector, or

      (c) a bona fide private education institution; such school must have a satisfactory record of enrolment and attendance at school of its students.

   (2) In addition he must show that he is able to and intends to

      (i) pursue a full time degree course if that is what he has been accepted for under (1)(a) above; or

      (ii) that his course of studies is a full-time course at an independent fee paying school if he has been accepted in such school under (1)(b) above. Such school must meet the requirements of the Education Act 1944 if the student is under 16 years of age. This requirement is to satisfy the authorities that such students under 16 are receiving full-time education as required by law and are not coming to pursue courses not prescribed under the said Education Act such as secretarial or other occupational courses; or

(iii) that his course is a weekday full-time one at a single institution and that he will attend a minimum of 15 hours organised daytime study per week for a single subject or directly related subjects under (1)(c) above. (This does not apply to those doing degree courses);

(3) that the student intends to leave the United Kingdom at the end of his studies (see also questions 48, 49 and 76);

(4) that he can, without working and without recourse to public funds, meet the cost of the course;

(5) that he can, without working and without recourse to public funds, meet the costs of his accommodation and that of any dependants;

(6) that he can, without taking employment and without recourse to public funds, meet the cost of his maintenance and that of any dependants.

The provision for not taking employment is qualified by an exception that such work is part-time or vacation work and is undertaken with consent of the Department of Employment.

Q.75   What proof will a student need to show the ECO or IO?

A.   He must satisfy the ECO or IO of all the requirements mentioned in the answer to question 74. What will be needed will be a formal letter from the school/college/university or polytechnic that he has been accepted, specifying the particular course, its duration, that it is a full time course, and that either full fees have been paid (preferably) or that a deposit has been made. In addition to these the student must provide evidence that either he is a government-sponsored student (in some cases the Ministry of Education or some governmental body will make his application and provide the relevant proof) or, if he is privately sponsored, that his sponsor (if sponsoring from the student's country) has the ability to pay all his fees for the course and also pay for all his maintenance and accommodation without recourse to public funds or work. This can be done by the production of the sponsor's bank statement and wage slips or other such evidence of his financial ability. All funds available abroad must be shown to be transferable. In certain cases where the student's wife has been permitted to work, her earnings may be counted.

With regards to fees, maintenance and accommodation, the student or his sponsor (if the sponsor is in United Kingdom) must show the accommodation available, that it is provided free by the sponsor or otherwise that there are adequate funds to pay for it without recourse to public funds or having to work, and that either the student or the sponsor has adequate funds to maintain the student without recourse to public funds or having to go to work. Proof of accommodation is by a letter from the health department of the local council stating that the accommodation is adequate or (if the house is being bought on a mortgage) a letter from the bank or building society that the premises are in the sponsor's possession and that he is allowed to take in the student. Evidence of means of maintenance by a sponsor should involve providing a bank statement or other evidence of earnings.

Q.76   How is intention to return assessed?

A.   It is vital that a student should intend to return at the end of his studies (*R v IAT ex parte Shaiku Murvin Ahmed* [1981] 1 WLR. 1107, *R v IAT ex parte Perween Khan* (1972) Imm.A.R. 268). The ECO or IO will want to know quite a lot and will ask all sorts of questions to establish this intention. He will want to know what benefit the course will be to the student in future, whether there are work opportunities in his country after qualifying (advertisements for such jobs showing the qualifications needed for them will be helpful), what his plans for the future are, whether he has relatives in the United Kingdom who came as students and where they are now (if the answer is 'yes' and they remained in the United Kingdom suspicion will be raised as to his following in the steps of such relatives), what relatives he has in his country, whether he is married, if he has children, whether they will go with him or stay behind, other commitments to the home country, and whether there is a business or job to go back to (evidence of such from the employer is helpful). The student may have various other reasons for not wishing to remain in the United Kingdom. He may be asked if he will look for suitable work in the United Kingdom after he has qualified and a 'yes' to this may have adverse effects on gaining entry.

It must be said that the grounds for refusing entry clearance or entry must be based on evidence and not mere suspicion (*ECO New Delhi v Bhambra* (1973) Imm.A.R. 14, see also question 48 above).

Q.77   What is meant by 'a full time course'?

A.   A full-time course, for the purpose of immigration, is one where the student has to do at least 15 hours daytime classes per week. If the student intends to do a course taking less than 15 hours per week it will be very difficult to get entry and so too if he intends to do two or more part-time courses totalling 15 or more hours per week. Under the new rules students are no longer permitted to enrol for a number of part-time courses at different establishments in order to make up the weekly 15 hours full-time studies. They must enrol for a single subject or, if more than one, then they must be directly related (for A-levels, for example) and should be in a single institution. This '15 hour requirement' means that a student studying two, three, or more subjects must have at least one subject on a full-time basis for at least 15 hours per week and the rest would be extra time. It does not apply to publicly funded institutions of higher learning (universities, or polytechnics) or full-time courses at an independent fee-paying school.

Q.78 Should the entry clearance applied for be for a specific course of a fixed duration?

A.   If this is the intention then the student applying must say so. If, however, he intends, for example, to do his O-levels or any particular course named and of a fixed duration but, when questioned, he states or it is found out that he will stay on to do his A-levels or other studies, he will be refused entry. On the other hand, if he shows that he is entering with a programme of studies in mind and says so, he will not be deemed to have an intention not to return home. He will, however, most likely be asked to state what the programme is and will have to apply for an extension at each stage and at the end of each period granted.

Q.79 Can a student come to do a vocational course if he is not proficient in English?

A.   Yes. The ECO or IO decides on granting or refusing a student visa or entry clearance or entry during the interview and this is when he takes into consideration the student's proficiency in English to see if he is able follow his course. The immigration tribunal has said that where a student coming to do a vocational course decides at the time of entry to follow an English language course first, this does not invalidate his entry clearance (if he has obtained one) (*re Pattuwearachchi (1991)* Imm.A.R. 341). A low standard of English should not be a hindrance if the student has satisfied the requirements of the course. He can gain by improving his English (*Sharma v SSHD* (1972) Imm.A.R. 219). The IO can contact the school to confirm acceptance in such cases (*Ashiq Husseinan* [1969] 3 All.ER 160). Such study must, however, satisfy the 15 hour per week rule or if the student is doing English only as a subsidiary subject then it must be in extra time.

Q.80 Can a student get entry to do a correspondence course in the United Kingdom?

A. Entry is not granted for normal courses to be taken by correspondence. The student can just as well do a correspondence course from his home country. In certain cases, such as journalism, where a correspondence course is also part of the course, it is allowed as this is one of the ways of getting qualified.

Q.81 What if he has not applied and been accepted to do a course and wishes to come as a prospective student?

A. A prospective student is one who has a genuine intention to study but has not made definite arrangements before travelling to the United Kingdom to look for a suitable course or to come for an interview with a particular institution. It is essential for the applicant to explain this and seek entry as such. He must also satisfy the other conditions, namely that he can maintain and accommodate himself (and any dependants) without recourse to public funds or working and can pay his fees and will return at the end of his studies, and that he will also show a realistic intention of entering into a course of study within six months of the date of his entry into the United Kingdom. The other requirements for a student entry as outlined above must also be capable of being met.

Q.82 What will be the next step for a prospective student if he gets entry to the United Kingdom?

A. He will be granted a short period of stay not exceeding six months to enable him to do what he came for. Once he has been accepted as a student on a full-time course he will then have to apply for a variation of his visa to that of a student and will then have to show his ability to continue to satisfy all the conditions that are required of a student as has been shown above.

Q.83 Can a prospective student apply for an extension of time?

A. Where such a student entered, having satisfied all the requirements mentioned, and was granted less than six months leave to remain, he can apply for an extension to enable him to complete his search for a course or institution. Such an extension may only be granted for the period remaining to make up the maximum period that he can be allowed, namely six months. If he was granted six months originally he cannot obtain any further time. An application to extend the period to make up the six months may have to be prepared to show what efforts he has made so far in finding a suitable course or educational institution.

Q.84 **Is it advisable for an intending student to apply for a visitor's visa and then apply to study when in the United Kingdom?**

A. Most definitely not! It is a dangerous course to take. A person coming to the United Kingdom with the intention of studying will best serve his purpose if he applied as a prospective student or a student (if he has made all the proper arrangements). If he does not do this and enters as a visitor and then enters into a course of study he would have breached the basis of his entry (as a visitor) and will be treated as an illegal entrant and removed quite quickly from the United Kingdom (*R v SSHD ex parte Adesina* (1988) Imm.A.R. 442, *R v SSHD ex parte Brakwah* (1989) Imm.A.R. 366). He may be considered to have obtained an entry clearance or entry by deception.

Another point to have in mind is that a visitor's visa cannot be longer than six months and a student's visa may be for the duration of the course. If the person entered from a visa country as a visitor or under any other category and wishes to apply to become a student he will have to return to his country and apply from there. It must also be noted that where deception has been used to enter it may be very difficult to obtain entry next time. Having said all this it is possible for someone not from a visa country who is already in the United Kingdom in some other category to apply to stay on for studies. This is a different position from one who comes in as a visitor or in some other category and then without applying to change goes on to undertake studies.

Q.85 **Who are classified as student nurses or midwives?**

A. They are persons who have been accepted to train in the United Kingdom as such (as student nurses or midwives or health visitors) where such training will result in a registered nursing or midwife qualification. If the person is already a nurse or midwife from overseas he may be accepted for an 'adaptation course' that will lead to that person becoming registered in the United Kingdom with the Central Council for Nursing, Midwifery and Health Visiting.

Q.86   **What are the requirements to train as a midwife or nurse?**

A.   At present the requirements for a student nurse or midwife are more
stringent than before October 1994 and are hardly any different from
ordinary students' requirements. He must show that he has been
accepted as a student nurse or trainee midwife, without any
misrepresentation, at a hospital or recognised nursing educational
establishment in the United Kingdom which meets the rules set by the
United Kingdom Central Council for Nursing, Midwifery and Health
Visiting. He must fall within the category of persons classified as
nurses or midwives as mentioned in the answer to the previous
question, and must be able to, and intend to, follow the course applied
for, and does not intend to work or engage in business, although
employment connected with his course may be allowed. He must have
sufficient funds for accommodation for himself and any dependants
without recourse to public funds or working (except as allowed).

He must show sufficient funds to maintain himself without recourse
to public funds or working. However, in this case, any bursary offered
by the Deptartment of Health can be considered in assessing whether
the student meets the maintenance requirement. He must intend to
leave Britain at the end of his course. The new rules, from October
1994, have made the days when such students enjoyed benefits like
free board and an allowance for maintenance after acceptance in a
training hospital with no need to show that they intended to return
home on completion of their studies, a thing of the past.

Q.87   **After qualifying as a nurse or midwife in the United Kingdom can he
then switch to work-permit employment?**

A.   No. Any such employment will have to be applied for through the
proper channel, namely the Department of Employment, by the
employing hospital or prospective employer.

Q.88   **What is the position of a qualified nurse or midwife who comes to the
United Kingdom for a visit and wishes to work?**

A.   She will normally be not be allowed to remain to work. She must
apply for a work permit through the employing hospital.

Q.89   **Can the wife or husband of a student be allowed to enter or join the other
spouse?**

A.   Yes. Students who have been admitted to the United Kingdom may be joined or accompanied by their spouses. There must be evidence of the marriage, of an intention to live together as spouses, that the marriage is subsisting, and that there is adequate maintenance and accommodation without recourse to public funds. (In this case the rules do not require 'exclusive accommodation'.) Intention to return at the end of the period granted must be shown. The period granted to the student will be the same as that granted to the spouse.

Q.90 Can the children of a student enter or join their student parent?

A. If such children are under 18 years, are not married, and have not formed an independent family unit, they will be admitted when both parents are in the United Kingdom. The new rules do not specify that both parents should be in the United Kingdom before the child can be allowed in. Presumably if one parent is abroad then unless the 'sole responsibility' rule applies to that parent abroad it would appear that the children can join the parent here.

Q.91 Can the mother of a student child be allowed to join him?

A. Where the child under 12 is granted leave to enter as a full-time private (fee-paying) student it is possible for the mother to be given extended leave to remain in order to look after her child. This concession is made on two conditions:

(i) that the father is living abroad, and

(ii) the mother's concession ceases when the child reaches 12 years.

If the mother has enough money to satisfy the rules under independent means (see the relevant section of this book) she can – before the child attains the age of 12 – apply to stay, and she can then bring in her husband and gain settlement in due course.

Q.92 What is 'the sole responsibility' rule?

A. For the answer to this see the section on settlement showing the requirements necessary – question 242 below.

Q93. Can a student take up employment during the course of his/her studies?

A. Normally this is not permissible. The entry was as a student and for full daytime studies of at least 15 hours a week. To take up employment he will need a work permit to be applied for by his employer and this will be contrary to the provisions of his original entry and the student can be prosecuted under the Immigration Act 1971 s24(1)*(b)*(i) or be deported.

There are circumstances when the student's course involves some work experience and training. In such cases the college applies for a training work permit to the Department of Employment Job Centre or makes arrangements with the firm taking the student on to apply for a permit to the Department of Employment. If this is not done the student may be in difficulties for working illegally. It is advisable in such cases for the student to make sure that his college has made this application.

Where the student wishes to take up part-time or vacation work not related to his course of studies he should check his passport to find out whether he had been 'prohibited' from working or 'restricted' from working. If the stamp is only a restriction he may get permission to work by applying to the Secretary of State for Employment for consent to do such work. If, on the other hand, the passport is stamped with a prohibition from working then he should apply to the Home Office to change it to a 'restriction', and at the same time make his application. This will only be granted if the HO is satisfied that the student does not need to work to be able to pay for his studies.

Whatever his circumstances, the student must not take up even short-term holiday work without compliance with procedure.

Q.94   Can the spouse of a student take up employment?

A.   The new rules specify that the spouse of a student must not intend to take up employment and that employment is prohibited. However, where the period of leave granted to the spouse is 12 months or more, then employment may be permitted.

Q.95   Can a student apply for extension of the period granted him?

A.   Yes. A student may be granted an extension for an appropriate period if such student can show that he is still enrolled as a full time day student and continues to meet all the requirements that he originally had to satisfy on entry. On application for an extension, the Home Office will make enquiries from the school/college or institution about attendance, fees, and also about the other requirements mentioned previously. A student must show regular attendance during his course. Attendance of 75 per cent is not considered satisfactory. Irregular attendance may be excused for good reasons such as illness (a medical report must be produced and sent to the Home Office with an explanation (*Hatjistefanou* (2617)). His lack of academic success in his course will also be considered (*in re Gerani* (1981) Imm.A.R. 187), and so will the taking and passing of the relevant examinations.

A student will be unlikely to get an extension if it will result in the student spending more than four years on short courses (courses of less than two years duration each or longer courses broken off before completion). If he is on scholarship – governmental or otherwise – and it has not come to an end, he will need a written acknowledgement of such continuation for the period applied for and evidence of sufficient funding by the sponsor/grantor. Any application for extension must be made before the expiry of the period granted him. He will become an overstayer the minute his original period to remain expires and can be removed from the United Kingdom. So long as he applies before the expiry date he can stay legally for as long as it takes the Home Office to decide.

Q.96 Can a student move from one course to another?

A. As shown in the answer to a previous question, this is frowned upon. When the student applied for entry he either gave a specific course of studies for which he was given entry, or obtained entry to embark upon 'a programme of studies'. The immigration authorities will not be unsympathetic if the student's courses follow a well-defined and acknowledged path to obtain his goal if the student moves from one course to another along this route. An O-level course followed by an A-level course leading to a course in law or medicine and so forth will normally be acceptable. A short course in drama to be followed by a short course in word processing to be followed by a short course in hair styling will not now fall within the requirement that a student enrol for a single subject or directly related subjects in the same institution. No longer is he allowed to enrol in a variety of part-time courses at different centres. He must continue as a *bona fide* student and not for an ulterior motive (*Karini re. D* 2423). Where there is a radical change of a course this must be given and with recommendations and letters from the tutors supporting the change, but all the previous requirements for the student entry will have to be satisfied and the time already taken in the previous course might also be relevant and a deliberate attempt by the student to extend his stay through such changes will not be considered favourably.

Q.97. Can an overseas student get a grant from the United Kingdom to study?

A. Overseas students normally have to pay full fees and are not entitled to local authority grants or awards. For a student from overseas to qualify as a 'home' student and pay the lower fees certain requirements must be met:

(i) he must have been ordinarily resident in the United Kingdom for at least three years before the course started. Certain exceptions may be made for those who cannot meet the three year period of ordinary residence because of temporary absence from the United Kingdom during all or part of the period;

(ii) he must not have been in the United Kingdom during the three years (minimum) period mentioned in (i) mainly or wholly for the purpose of full time education.

Those who have been here for three years as students will not qualify.

Those allowed into the United Kingdom for other reasons, for example children of work-permit holders or those who have obtained settlement (indefinite leave to remain) but who were students during that time, can apply for the lower 'home' student fees for new courses. Those granted refugee status or exceptional leave to remain (after making a claim for asylum) can pay the lower fees even though they have not been here for three years.

Those waiting for decisions on their asylum claims are not entitled to a grant.

Q.98   **What is the position of a trainee?**

A.   There are circumstances when the student's course involves some work experience and training. In such cases the college applies to the Department of Employment Jobcentre for a training work permit or makes arrangements with the firm taking the student on to apply for a permit to the Department of Employment. If this is not done the student may be in difficulties for working illegally.

It is advisable in such cases for the student to make sure that his college has done this. If he wishes to enter in order to train for any employment not involving a student's course then see the section under 'trainees'.

Q.99   **Can a student change his immigration status?**

A.   Yes.

(i) A student may marry and apply to stay with his/her spouse if such spouse is settled or is a British citizen. This will be subject to certain requirements relating to marriage for which see the section on settlement (marriage).

(ii) A student whose parents or close relatives have gained settlement may apply to stay and settle with them.

(iii) A student cannot now apply to stay as a working holiday-maker (see section on working holidaymakers): under the new rules an entry clearance for this category should be applied for. This implies that any application to change from student to working holidaymaker will be refused.

(iv) A student can apply for asylum.

(v) A student can apply to become a visitor for a short period at the end of his studies.

(vi) A student cannot stay in order to work.

(vii) A student cannot stay to set up business or be self employed, or as a person of independent means.

(vii) A student cannot stay to became an au pair.

(ix) A student cannot become settled because he has been in the United Kingdom as such for a long period. Extension of a stay will not be granted where this will entail staying on for more than four years on short courses (courses lasting less than two years' duration or longer courses broken off before completion). If the course entails continuation over four years then it may be possible to obtain indefinite leave to remain after four years' continuous stay.

All applications for a change of status must be made before the end of the period of the student's leave to remain.

Q.100 Can a student stay in the United Kingdom after he has completed his studies?

A. Only with permission. Students who wish to remain after their formal studies for a degree-granting ceremony or to write a thesis for their PhD or similar degree should apply in time, before the end of the period granted them, and have the support of the college or university. They must be able to continue to accommodate and support themselves without need of public support. Where a student has been in the United Kingdom for close on 10 years and then applies for such extension this might be looked upon with suspicion due to the Home Office policy of granting a 'concession' to settle after 10 years (see question 261).

Q.101 Can a student travel out of the United Kingdom during the period granted him to remain?

A.   Students can travel out of the United Kingdom and return within the time limit of their leave to remain whether visa-nationals or not provided that their study period was longer than six months. If their period of study was for less than six months they must reapply in the country they are visiting for a new visa before they can return unless they had previously obtained multiple visas. It must be pointed out that students, wherever they come from, must not take it for granted that they will be readmitted into United Kingdom after any absence. The IO may need to be satisfied before every entry and it is therefore advisable to obtain a letter from the educational institution confirming that studies are continuing, proof of their financial support and accommodation to be shown on their return.

Q.102 What is the position if a student wishes to study to be a barrister?

A.   The same rules for entry apply to him as would apply to any other student. In the case of the Bar he will have to register with the Council of Legal Education as a student. The academic stage must first be completed. If he is a United Kingdom graduate with a minimum of second class (ii)(Hons) degree in law he can then apply for membership of one of the Inns of Court. If he holds a non-law United Kingdom degree with second class (ii)(Hons), or an overseas law or non-law degree, he must do a one year Common Professional Examination, and a one year law conversion course, then he can apply to become a member of an Inn. In some cases non-graduate mature students with a Common Professional Examination will do a two year law conversion course and then apply to become a member of an Inn. After the academic stage comes the vocational stage. No student can start the Bar vocational course unless he has become a member of one of the four Inns of Court – Inner Temple, Middle Temple, Lincoln's Inn, Gray's Inn.

For the Inner Temple, and quite probably for the other Inns, overseas students who are not reading for a degree in the United Kingdom must obtain a written recommendation from the Education Department of his home country or from the officer in charge of student affairs in his Embassy/High Commission in the United

Kingdom. If he has been a student in the United Kingdom for two years or more he will need a character certificate from his tutor.

After registration as a member of an Inn he will register at the Inns of Court School of Law and do a one-year vocational training course if he intends to practise at the Bar (in which case he would have to obtain immigration status), and if he does not intend to practise here he will do a Bar Examination Course of one year and will not qualify for any scholarship or bursary. Before sitting for the Bar examinations a student must have dined nine times in hall but before being called to the Bar (after going through all the examinations) he should have completed 18 dinners. Once the student has completed the vocational stage and has been called, or is about to be called, to the Bar then he will have to do 'pupillage' – a sort of apprenticeship under a registered 'pupil-master' in chambers. This pupillage is divided into two six-month periods. The first is the non-practising six and the next the practising six when he can represent clients. During his pupillage he will have to do a professional development course consisting of an 'advocacy' course and an 'advice to counsel' course (very short two-day courses) which (since September 1992) form a standard part of pupillage. The above is just an insight into what the student intending to study to be a Barrister here must be prepared for (the 'programme of studies' that he will be embarking upon, the length of time, accommodation, maintenance, and finances to be prepared for in order to be able to satisfy the immigration officer or visa officer to obtain entry).

After qualifying here or abroad, if he wishes to set up practice in the United Kingdom as a foreign lawyer then there are further immigration requirements governing his stay here to practise (see question 72).

Q.103 What are the requirements to study to become a solicitor?

A.   The same rules apply to him for entry as would apply to any other student.

To study to become a solicitor there are three routes open to the student:

(1) the law graduate route;

(2) the non-law graduate route; and

(3) the non-graduate (legal executive) route.

Under (1) the student should have three passes with good grades (c) in the A-level GCE. Thereafter the student takes a law degree. The student must cover the 'core' subjects required by both the Law Society (solicitors) and the Inns of Court (barristers). These subjects are constitutional and administrative law, contract, tort, criminal law, land law and equity and trusts. After obtaining a law degree the next stage is the legal practice course. When the academic course is completed, the student joins the Law Society. A full-time legal practice course runs for one year and a part-time one goes on for two years and covers subjects like wills, probate, conveyancing, and so forth. After completing the legal practice course the student will be required to spend two years in a training contract working in paid employment under a solicitor. This period will include a professional skills course (accounts, professional conduct and so forth). This will be a period of training and the applicant will not be considered a student any longer for immigration purposes and thus a foreign student will have to obtain Department of Employment approval as a trainee.

Under (2) there is a requirement for A-level subjects followed by a degree course which is not a law degree, and the student will thereafter be required to obtain a Certificate of Eligibility from the Law Society in order to do a one-year full-time course or two-year part time course leading to the Common Professional Examination (which covers the six 'core' subjects) in order to familiarise him with law subjects. This is followed by the legal practice course and the training contract and professional skills course, as mentioned before.

Under (3) the student may either have GCSE (four subjects with good passes) or be a mature student over 25 years of age. He will then enter legal employment and register with the Institute of Legal Executives and do a course (employment requires Department of Employment approval). Part one takes one to two years and part two (including any three of the core subjects) also takes one to two years and the examinations (considered as the academic stage) will make the student a Member of the Institute of Legal Executives (MILEX). He must be over 25, with five years in legal employment (preferably in the United Kingdom and this would have implied a work permit) and must have served two years after becoming a MILEX. This is then followed by further examinations to become a Fellow of the Institute of Legal Executives (FILEX), involving the remaining three core subjects. After successfully obtaining the FILEX he then registers as a student member of the Law Society and attends the legal practice course. There will then be no requirement to enter a training contract in a solicitors' firm but the student will have to take the professional skills course before being admitted as a solicitor.

The above is just an insight into what the student intending to study to be a solicitor here must be prepared for. After qualifying here, if the applicant wishes to set up practice in the United Kingdom as a foreign lawyer then there are further immigration requirements governing his stay here to practise as has been shown above.

Chapter 5

People entering on business

Although this chapter contains questions on self-employed people and business people, I have added certain categories which have been classified under the rules as those seeking entry as sole representatives of businesses; representatives of newspapers, news agencies, broadcasting organisations; airline ground staff at airports in the United Kingdom for the sake of convenience and because they form part and parcel of 'business' and are connected with the setting up of business in the United Kingdom, albeit as employed representatives of businesses abroad. These are permit-free workers.

BUSINESSMEN AND SELF-EMPLOYED PEOPLE

Q.104 Does someone coming to the United Kingdom to set up a business or to become self-employed need an entry clearance?

A. Yes. A businessman, or someone coming here for self-employment, must have a prior entry clearance/visa before coming to the United Kingdom, irrespective of which country he is coming from. To obtain this he must satisfy the entry clearance officer (or visa officer) in his country that he can meet the various requirements set out in the question and answer below.

Q.105 What must be shown to the ECO?

A. A businessman coming to set up a new business must show that:

(i) He has £200 000 clear capital of his own to use for setting up the new business.* The money must not be borrowed (*R v SSHD ex parte Peikazadi* (no. 2027) (1979–80) Imm.A.R. 191) and not held in trust. The money must be under his complete control and must be disposable by him in the United Kingdom (*re Mehra* (no.2499)).

(ii) He will be occupied full time in the business and will not be occupied for long periods outside the United Kingdom. His business in the United Kingdom must need him.

(iii) His business will create new employment for at least two people in the United Kingdom.* These jobs must be an on-going and permanent feature of the business and not jobs that will need a succession of independent contractors (*Sayed* (no. 5006) (1987) Imm.A.R. 303).

(iv) He can support and accommodate himself and his dependants, without having to use money from the £200 000 business capital* and thereby diminishing that capital, and without working outside his business, and without recourse to public funds. This implies having in excess of the £200 000, such excess to be used for accommodation and maintenance for himself and his dependants whilst the business is being established without having to call upon public funds or being employed himself to supplement his business. Thereafter he must show that the profits from the business can accommodate and maintain him and his dependants without recourse to public funds or employment.

(v) His interest in the business must be commensurate with his financial investment. It will seem suspicious if, for example, in a partnership, he has a 60 per cent interest when his level of investment is only 40 per cent.

(vi) There must be a genuine need for his investing in business in the United Kingdom. This normally will depend on the prospect for employing workers, whether his business will generate tax returns, the type of services his business will render to the public, and other considerations.

(vii) He will be able to bear his financial liabilities.

(viii) Any partnership in a new business must not amount to a disguised employment. The applicant must have a genuine equal interest or a controlling interest in the business.

* The Home Office may agree to accept a sum less than this amount as an investment if the business will generate employment for more than the minimum two employees. It is advisable to consult an adviser on this subject.

Q.106 **What type of business can a businessman set up in the United Kingdom?**

A.   He can set up either as a sole trader or as a partner in a new or existing business, or as a registered company.

Q.107 Are there different requirements where the businessman intends to join as a partner or take over an existing business in the United Kingdom?

A.   Yes. In addition to those requirements mentioned in the questions above (questions 104 and 105) he must produce a written statement showing the terms and conditions of the partnership or takeover as well as an audited account of the business for the previous years. In addition he must show that his services and investment will increase the full-time employment figure of the business by a minimum of two over what it is at the time of becoming a partner or of the take-over and obtain an entry clearance as a partner or as one taking over an existing business.

Q.108 In considering the minimum amount, can an applicant's house in the United Kingdom be counted towards this sum?

A.   No. The value of any freehold property that he possesses in the United Kingdom will not be considered favourably in satisfying the financial requirement (*Hussain Rahman* (7379)), although if the house will be for his own use this will satisfy the accommodation requirement, depending on the size of the house and the number of dependants he may have.

Q.109 What if he inherits a business already in the United Kingdom worth over the required amount?

A.   He will not have satisfied the rules if he simply inherits a business worth £200 000 or more in the United Kingdom.

Q.110 What is meant by 'money or funds under his control'?

A.   This means he has the right of full control over the money and that he can enforce such rights in law against anyone who may wish to interfere with it.

Q.111 How long will a businessman be allowed to stay in the United Kingdom?

A.   He will be given an initial period of one year, which may be extended to four years in all, provided that he applies to extend the period before the end of the initial period.
        He will have to demonstrate that the investment of £200 000 of his

own money has been made, that the business is continuing, that at least two new jobs have been created, that he is not working for someone else and has not had recourse to public funds, and that his share in business profits can maintain and accommodate him. In fact he will have to show that everything required of him as mentioned above in question 105 has been complied with and is still being complied with.

Q.112   Can a businessman extend his stay after the four years?

A.   Before the end of the four-year period mentioned in the answer to question 111 he may then apply (before the expiry of the period) for settlement or for a further term. He will again have to show that the business is continuing and that it is supporting him and his dependants (if any) and, in fact, show all over again that he has satisfied and continues to satisfy all the requirements in the answers to questions 104 and 105.

He must also show that he has been in the United Kingdom for a continuous period of four years in the capacity in which he first entered and must submit audited accounts for the first three years of trading, and a management account for the last year.

Q.113   Can he, whilst in the United Kingdom as a businessman, take up employment abroad?

A.   No. He must not have any employment here or abroad at any time. This will defeat the requirements of being in full-time employment on his firm's business.

Q.114   Can a businessman bring in his spouse and family?

A.   Yes. Generally, the spouse and any unmarried children under 18 who have not formed an independent family unit will be given entry for the same period as the applicant provided he satisfies all the requirements for support and accommodation. This latter requirement now calls for the parent to own or occupy such accommodation exclusively (shared accommodation with non-family members will not be acceptable). This unreasonable requirement may be altered as a result of the increase in the shortage of housing and pressure by immigration groups. The spouse and family must also have an entry clearance or an appropriate visa before accompanying or joining the businessman. After four years he can apply for settlement for himself and for his family.

Q.115 Can the spouse and children take up employment in the United Kingdom?

A.   Yes. Generally this will depend on whether their passports were stamped with a 'prohibition' from working or a 'restriction' on working. If it is the former then they cannot take up employment but if it is the latter they may. Normally, if a stay is granted over 12 months, then employment may be allowed.

Q.116 Can he change his status from that of businessman to any other category?

A.   Yes. He can change to a 'spouse' if he marries a British citizen or someone with settlement rights. He will be given a year's leave initially and he may apply before the end of that year for settlement status. He may apply to become a refugee or an asylum seeker. After four years stay as a businessman he can apply to become settled. If he is not a visa national he can apply to be a student. If he is a visa national he will have to leave the country and apply from abroad to become a student, as we have seen. He cannot change to be an au pair if he is from the countries specified (see section under 'au pair'). He can change to visitor at the end of his stay as a businessman but only for a short period. He will not be granted variation of his status if he applies to become a working holidaymaker, or to stay only in his capacity as fiancé, or to change to a work-permit holder to take up employment.

Q.117 Can he get settlement?

A.   He can apply to settle after four years continuous stay (see further down) in the United Kingdom as a businessman. He will again have to show that the business is continuing and is supporting him and his dependants (if any) and, in fact, show all over again that he has satisfied and continues to satisfy all the requirements in the answer to questions 104 and 105, and also show that he has been in the United Kingdom for a continuous period of four years in the capacity he first entered as, and submit audited accounts for the first three years of trading, and a management account for the last year.

Normally the Home Office will not consider reasonable periods of absence from the United Kingdom, such as vacations, or business trips, or short family visits, as breaching the 'continuous residence' rule. There is no hard and fast rule and if he has maintained his base in the United Kingdom and can show good reason for his going abroad it should not count against the requirement that he be continuously resident in the United Kingdom. He can also apply for his spouse and children under 18 or other dependants to get settlement. This will be on the conditions already mentioned above (question 105). If he is not married when he entered, then marrying a British citizen will, if he satisfies the rules as to marriage, enable him to obtain settlement.

Q.118 Are there differences between coming as a businessman or coming as self-employed ?

A.   There are, but only very slight. The 'self-employed' category includes those wishing to set up as professionals such as architects, doctors in private practice, accountants. The requirements are more or less the same as those of businessmen.

Lawyers have a special category that does not have the same requirements.

Writers, artists and composers also have their own categories with their own requirements. These other self-employed categories will be dealt with below.

REPRESENTATIVES OF OVERSEAS FIRMS

Q.119 Can a representative of an overseas firm with no branch or subsidiary in the United Kingdom be allowed to set up as such in the United Kingdom?

A.   Yes. An entry clearance/visa must be obtained specifically for that purpose. The firm abroad must be in existence and have no subsidiary or other representative in the United Kingdom. The applicant must also show the minutes appointing him as the firm's representative, why he is the best person, and his expertise. He must be recruited abroad. He will not need a work permit to set up a branch but others who may come to work for the branch will need work permits. His position must be that of a senior employee with power to make decisions about the operation of the company on behalf of the overseas firm. The branch here must be registered as a branch or a wholly-owned subsidiary of the overseas company. His employment here must be full time and he must not hold a majority of the shares in that firm. He must be able to accommodate and maintain himself and dependants without recourse to public funds or employment except within the scope of his appointment as a representative.

Apart from the usual business representation, there are rules for representatives of overseas newspapers, news agencies and broadcasting organisations, and airlines, all mentioned below.

There is also a new type of 'sole representative' category for those based abroad but making frequent or lengthy trips, who do not qualify as ordinary visitors nor as full time representatives. People wishing to enter as such must seek further advice on this aspect.

Q.120 What are the requirements for representatives of overseas newspapers, news agencies and broadcasting organisations?

A. The representative must be currently engaged by the overseas newspaper, agency or organisation and must be posted to the United Kingdom on a long-term assignment. He will work in full-time employment only for the employers abroad. This entails not taking up any other employment apart from that involved in his work for that overseas newspaper, agency or broadcasting organisation. The other normal requirements, that he should adequately maintain and accommodate himself and his dependants without recourse to public funds, also apply. He must obtain an entry clearance from his country to enter as a representative. This category is permit free.

Q.121 How long can such representative be allowed to stay?

A. He will be given an initial period of 12 months. After this period he can extend the stay, provided he has applied before the expiration of this 12 months. In such a case he will have to show that he is still required and is still engaged by his employers in the same category as he entered, that he still intends to work full time and will not take up other employment and can still maintain and accommodate himself and his dependants without recourse to public funds. Where all these requirements are satisfied he will be granted an extension of a further three years.

Q.122 What are the requirements for overseas airlines employees?

A. Setting up a branch in the United Kingdom follows the normal routine application but where the airline operating from the United Kingdom needs to send operational ground staff then an application for entry clearance must be made and the following requirements will have to be satisfied: the applicant will have been transferred to the United Kingdom by the overseas-owned airline operating services to and from the United Kingdom. He will have to take up duty in an international airport either as station manager, or security manager, or technical manager and will be working full-time for the employers and will not take up other employment apart from that for which he had gained admission. Adequate maintenance and accommodation should be available without recourse to public funds. This category is also a permit-free employment.

Q.123 How long will an airline representative be given to stay in the United Kingdom?

A.   The usual initial 12 months will be given and, if followed by an application made before the expiry of this period, then he may be granted a further three years, before the end of which period he may again apply to extend his stay.

Q.124 Can the representative of either an overseas airline or a newspaper or news agency or broadcasting organisation get indefinite leave to remain in the United Kingdom?

A.   Yes. In any of these cases the representative may obtain indefinite leave to remain if he has spent a continuous period of four years in the same category as he entered and has satisfied all the requirements needed as set out in the relevant category above and is still needed for that employment. A certificate from his employers to show such need is necessary. This is permit-free employment. Continuous periods of stay in the United Kingdom has been dealt with in a previous answer.

WRITERS, COMPOSERS AND ARTISTS

Q.125 What are the requirements for writers, composers and artists?

A.   They must apply for an entry clearance. To obtain this they must have established themselves outside the United Kingdom as either writers, composers or artists depending on which category they are applying for. They must have published original works (but such works do not include articles or publications in newspapers or magazines if they are writers) or must have published or performed original musical opera or exhibited artistic works of a literary, musical or artistic merit. Their intention in coming to the United Kingdom must be to become self-employed in pursuit of their writings or art or musical compositions and not for employment under others. They must show that in the preceding year they have been able to maintain themselves and their dependants from their own works as a writers or composers or artists and that on entry to the United Kingdom they will be able to maintain and accommodate themselves and any dependants without recourse to public funds.

Q.126 What period of stay will a writer, composer or artist be allowed?

A. Like all the others mentioned above, he will get an initial period of up to 12 months. If he wishes to have an extension of this period he can, before the expiry of the initial period, apply for such extension. He will have to show that he continues to satisfy all the requirements for entry and stay as mentioned above. He may then be given a further three years leave to remain. This process for extension may be repeated for a further period.

If he wishes to apply for indefinite leave to remain then, before the end of the fourth year, he must apply for such leave and go through the same procedure of showing that he has been here for a continuous period of four years and has continued to satisfy all the requirements. Professional artists who exhibit or work internationally and travel frequently to the United Kingdom can have 'season ticket' permits, so lightening the requirement of having to apply on different occasions for engagements in the United Kingdom. This will cover trips abroad for up to a year.

Amateur artists, and those individuals attending major approved festivals (such as the Notting Hill Carnival) can be allowed in permit-free as visitors. So can entertainers (see above under visitors – entertainers/film crews).

Q.127 What do the terms 'writers', 'artists', 'composers' include?

A. The terms 'writers' and 'artists' include authors, script-writers, painters (in the sense of art painting), sculptors, and commercial artists. 'Composers' mainly refer to those who compose music. It was held in one case that a composer of music is a writer. 'A writer of books, a writer of plays ... of script ... of nonsense, ... of real sense ... all come within the meaning of writer' (R v IAT ex parte Ahart (1981) Imm.A.R. 76).

It was also held that writing 'includes journalism, freelance or otherwise, editing, consultancy, public relations' (in re Shevey (case no. 5160) (1987) Imm.A.R. 453). However it is not now clear that these last categories fall under the new rules which require a separate entry clearance if coming to the United Kingdom as a representative of a newspaper, news agency, or broadcasting organisation. If coming here for employment then a work permit is needed, or if coming as an independent businessman to set up such a career then an entry clearance is needed for that category.

Artistes, actors, musicians, dancers, and singers and photographers (except perhaps art photographers) are not included. These will have to get work permits if they wish to enter to perform (SSHD v Stillwagon (1975) Imm.A.R. 132). A composer who composes his own songs and lyrics and sings them will still be considered as a composer and therefore will not require a work permit.

Q.128 As writers, artists and composers are classified as 'self-employed' will they need to have £200 000 ?

A.   These categories are exempt from this particular financial require-ment. As shown above, they will have to satisfy only the requirements mentioned in question 125.

Q.129 Can the spouse and children of writers, composers or artists be allowed to accompany or join them?

A.   Yes. The writer, composer or artist whose spouse is accompanying or joining him must be married and the marriage must be subsisting. They must intend to live together as man and wife. Adequate accommodation and maintenance for the spouse and children should be available without recourse to public funds. The accommodation must be owned or occupied exclusively by them. The spouse and children must intend to leave the United Kingdom at the end of any period granted to the applicant spouse (in other words to the writer/composer/artist). An entry clearance must be obtained before coming. Children accompanying the writer, composer or artist must be under 18, unmarried and must not have formed separate family units or live independent lives. The requirement for accommodation and main-tenance is the same as mentioned. The period of stay will not exceed that granted the parents. Both parents must have been admitted to stay in the United Kingdom. Where only one was admitted, a child will be admitted only if the parent admitted to the United Kingdom has sole responsibility for the child's upbringing or there are serious family or other considerations that will make the child acceptable to enter or remain with the parent here. Suitable arrangements for the child's care and upbringing must have been made. The child or children must have obtained a valid entry clearance before coming.

Q.130 Can the writer or composer or artist and his spouse and children be allowed to remain indefinitely?

A.   Yes, if they all had valid entry clearance to enter or remain in their capacity as writer, composer or artist or spouse or child. If the applicant and his family wish to apply for indefinite leave to remain then, before the end of the fourth year, he must apply for such leave and go through the same procedure, showing that he has been here for a continuous period of four years (see questions 112 and 117) and has continued to satisfy all the requirements. Indefinite leave to remain can only be gained by the spouse and children if the application by the writer, composer or artist succeeds.

INVESTORS

Q.131 Who is regarded as an investor?

A. This is a new category introduced under the new rules which came into effect on 1 October 1994. An investor must have no less than £1 million under his control and disposable in the United Kingdom. (Where the money is not transferable from abroad without exchange control permits such money may not be considered to be freely under his control. Obtaining previous permission to transfer may help in this direction.) He must invest at least £750 000 of this capital in the United Kingdom. Investments can only be in the form of government bonds, share capital, or loan capital in United Kingdom registered companies involved in active trading. Such investments cannot be made with property investment companies, or as bank deposits, or deposits with building societies, or any similar company whose business is to take money on deposit or in unit trusts. Indications are that a small investment of about 10 per cent of the total of his money may be allowed if invested in property. There is no age limitation or restriction on an investor apart from being above 18. He may take self-employment. He may even be allowed to invest in his own company if such company is not one that will make investment prohibited under this category.

Q.132 What other requirements must an investor satisfy?

A. Apart from the financial requirements he must intend to make the United Kingdom his main home. This does not mean his permanent home and the investor may have a second home abroad and may visit for social or business reasons, but the United Kingdom must be his main base and he must spend a far greater proportion of his time (about nine months) in the United Kingdom if he wishes to apply for indefinite leave in due course. He must be able to accommodate and maintain himself and any dependants adequately and without taking up employment and without recourse to public funds. He can become self-employed or set up business but these activities will have to have the consent of the Secretary of State. His passport will be stamped with a restriction on his right to take up other types of employment.

He must apply for entry clearance abroad to come in as an intending investor and must show the entry clearance officer that he is in a position to carry out all the requirements. It is the Home Office and not the ECO who will consider the application.

Q.133 How long will an investor be allowed to stay?

A.   The initial period will be for 12 months and if he wishes an extension he must apply before the end of the 12 months. The Home Office will then want to have proof all over again that he entered with a valid entry clearance in the category of an investor, and that all the other requirements mentioned above are satisfied (as if he is newly entering the country) including showing that he has made the United Kingdom his main home. He will then be granted a further three years with the same restriction on employment. The same period will be given to his spouse and children if he has applied for them and if they hold valid entry clearance. They should have no restrictions on taking employment.

Q.134 Can he and his spouse and children obtain indefinite leave to remain?

A.   Yes. If the investor applies for indefinite leave to remain with his family he will be granted such leave if he can show he has been in the United Kingdom continuously for four years and has met the requirements of the rules as mentioned in questions 132 and 133. As one of the requirements is his intention to make the United Kingdom his main home this leave for indefinite stay would be expected. 'Continuous residence' has been mentioned above in previous answers. He will also have to show that the spouse and children had valid entry clearances and (as in the case for applying for such clearance) that the children are under 18, that the investor and his spouse live together, that the marriage is subsisting, and that there will be adequate exclusive accommodation and maintenance without recourse to public funds.

ECAA BUSINESSMEN

Q.135 What are the requirements for those from the ECAA wishing to establish a business in the United Kingdom?

The ECAA stands for the European Community Association Agreement and came into force in the European Union on 1 February

1994. The requirements will depend on whether the entrant is coming (A) to establish himself in a company registered in the United Kingdom which he effectively controls or (B) to establish himself in self-employment (as a sole trader) or in partnership in the United Kingdom:

In the former case (A) he will need to show that:

(i) he is a national of Hungary or Poland (see ** below);

(ii) the money he is investing in the business is completely under his control and is sufficient to establish him in business in the United Kingdom. In the rules no specified amount is set for this venture;

(iii) apart from the money he is putting into the business he must have sufficient money to maintain and accommodate himself and any dependants without recourse to public funds or to employment until his business or his controlling share in the business provides him with an income enough to provide these requirements;

(iv) he must not have any intention of seeking employment to supplement his income.

All these requirements must be proved to the entry clearance officer to be sustainable. Then he can get an entry clearance for this specific purpose after consideration by the Home Office. He will also have to show that:

(v) he will be actively involved in managing and promoting the company;

(vi) the company is registered in the United Kingdom; and

(vii) such company is the owner of the assets of the business (in other words that such assets are not owned by him personally).

If he is taking over an existing company in the United Kingdom then he must

(viii) show a written statement of all the terms on which the takeover is based as well as

(ix) an audited account for the previous years.

Where the applicant is Hungarian he will have the same benefits as a

Polish applicant after five years.

** Since 1995, citizens of Bulgaria, the Czech Republic, Romania and Slovakia have come under a European Community Agreement and can also establish as sole traders or in a partnership or to form a company that they effectively control under paragraphs 211-223 of the Rules.

In the case (B) (as sole trader or in partnership) he must be a national of Poland or of the new states mentioned above and must be able to meet the requirements numbered A (i) – (v) above, and will be actively involved in providing services on his own account (if in self-employment) or in partnership (if he enters as a partner). He (or his partners) must be the owners of all the assets of the business, and his part of the business, if a partnership, will be as a genuine partner and not be a disguise for employment. If he is taking over an existing company in the United Kingdom he must show a written statement of the terms on which the takeover is based and an audited account for the previous years.

The minimum investment of £200 000 is not required in these cases, nor is there the requirement to show that full-time employment will be created in the United Kingdom for at least two people.

Q.136 How long will any of the above businessmen be granted to stay in the United Kingdom?

A.   If, on arrival, he holds an entry clearance he may be granted up to but not exceeding 12 months in either case A or B above. If he requires a further extension then he must make his application before the end of the initial period granted him and show that he continues to satisfy all the requirements in his case (whether as a registered company or as a sole trader or partnership).

He may apply for indefinite leave to remain if this has been granted and if he has remained for four years in the United Kingdom in the same capacity as he entered and is still engaged in the business, provided he has continued to satisfy all the requirements in his case and provides audited accounts for the first three years and a management account for the fourth year.

Chapter 6

Working in the United Kingdom

Some occupations need a work permit and others do not. Those needing permits are dealt with by the Department of Employment and those not needing permits are dealt with by the immigration authorities. The latter occupations are known as 'permit-free' employment and the employers need not apply to the Department of Employment for work permits. There are other categories not needing work permits, such as representatives of overseas newspapers, news agencies, and broadcasting organisations, but these have been dealt with elsewhere (under 'businesses'). On application for entry clearance, the Embassy/High Commission may refer the matter to the Home Office here for confirmation of the details of the jobs. A fee is payable for the entry clearance (or for a visa in the case of visa-nationals). Those considered to be within the categories needing work permit are dealt with in questions 137 to 150. The rest do not need work permits.

EMPLOYMENT / WORK PERMITS

Q.137 What requirement should someone coming to the United Kingdom to seek employment meet?

A.   So long as he is not a seaman under contract coming to join a ship in the United Kingdom that is leaving the United Kingdom, and that he is otherwise eligible under the immigration rules to seek employment in the United Kingdom (in other words, he is of United Kingdom ancestry), he should hold a valid work permit issued by the Department of Employment in the United Kingdom. He must not be outside the age limit for employment. At the moment women over 60 and men over 65 are entitled to retirement. Earlier age limits of between 23 and 54 for overseas nationals no longer apply.

   The applicant must show that he does not intend to do any work apart from that defined in the work permit and must be able to carry out such work. The other general requirements for this and all other categories are that he must be able to adequately accommodate and maintain himself and any dependant granted leave to enter, without recourse to public funds. If the work permit is valid only for 12 months or less he must intend to leave the United Kingdom at the end of his approved employment.

Q.138 Does such a person need a prior entry clearance?

A.   The rules do not require this if he is not a visa national but it is always advisable to obtain one. The person concerned must be sure that his prospective employers have applied for a work permit and he must make sure that it is a genuine work permit issued by the Department of Employment in the United Kingdom and that all the facts put forward are true. If the applicant used deception or false representation or did not disclose a material fact, even though it was without the knowledge of the work permit holder, then entry could be refused. An example is where the employers applied but the worker was not capable of doing the job. Always check with the Department of Employment here for validity of the permit before applying to enter.

It is advisable to apply for a visa or entry clearance to enter. As I have mentioned in Chapter 1 above, if an entrant has in his possession an entry clearance or visa it will make his entry easier here and give him a right of appeal against refusal of entry whilst he is on United Kingdom soil. One must either satisfy the ECO abroad or the IO in the United Kingdom and it is always safer and cheaper to be refused from home than from here. In any case, so long as a valid work permit has been obtained and the other requirements can be met then there should be no problems. Employees from Commonwealth countries receive their work permits through the High Commission in their country so an entry clearance should not be difficult to obtain. Other nationals receive theirs through their employers (*R v IO ex parte Chan* [1992] 2 All ER 738 applying *Khan v SSHD* [1977] 3 All ER 538).

Q.139 Are there any categories of workers eligible for work permits?

A.   Those with professional qualifications, executive or administrative staff, highly trained technicians with specialised qualifications, those with qualifications not easily found amongst workers, experienced workers in hotel or catering work with certificates of at least two years' full-time training or with uncommon skills, some sportsmen and entertainers. The Secretary of State may allow anyone in, in the national interest, whom he considers suitably qualified. Entrants should normally have an adequate knowledge of English.

Q.140 What is the age qualification for workers?

A.   Formerly the employee had to be between 23 and 54 except for sportsmen and entertainers when the age limit could be varied. However the Department of Employment has reviewed this and the requirement for overseas nationals no longer applies.

Q.141 Can a worker change his employment after entering Britain?

A. Leave to enter is subject to restrictions on other employment and before he may change employment the worker will need the consent of the Department of Employment. He cannot engage in business or a profession without the consent of the Home Office. He must not intend to take up employment other than as specified and any change of employment may make an application for extension refusable.

Q.142 How long will the work permit holder be given to stay?

A. If his original leave was only for 12 months or less he may be given a further three years extension. He must apply to the Home Office before the end of the original period. The Home Office may then grant the extension as mentioned. If his work permit was for over 12 months the Home Office will refer the matter to the Department of Employment for it to approve the continuation of the employment. Normally he can stay up to but not exceeding four years.

Q.143 Can he obtain indefinite leave to stay?

A. Yes, if he has spent a continuous period of four years as a work permit holder and has, throughout, satisfied all the requirements, including that of obtaining the Department of Employment's certificate stating that he has their approval for the continuation of his work, that he is still needed in his employment, and that he is adequately accommodated and maintained without recourse to public funds.

Q.144 Can he bring his spouse and children?

A. Yes. His spouse and children under 18 may be allowed to accompany or join him provided they can be housed and maintained without recourse to public funds. Entry clearances will be required.

Approved training or work experience

Q.145 What are the requirements to enter as a trainee or to obtain work experience?

A. These categories fall under schemes approved by the Department of Employment in the United Kingdom. The person wishing to enter as a trainee or to obtain work experience must apply for and obtain placement from the employer. The employer should have applied for and obtained a permit from the Department of Employments stating that such employer is offering a genuine training project or work experience which is not available in the trainee's country or in the country of the person seeking work experience. However the Department of Employment has said that applications where the overseas national is already qualified in his home country can be considered where training is involved. The trainee or person seeking work experience must not be of an age that places him outside the limit for employment. He must have the ability to understand and perform the job. Other requirements are that he must be able to accommodate and maintain himself and any dependants adequately without recourse to public funds and that he must intend to leave the United Kingdom at the end of the period granted. In this case there is no mention in the rules that the accommodation must be exclusively for the use of the trainee or person seeking work experience and so that person may share accommodation. However, if he wishes to bring any dependants with him, or to join him, the rules call for exclusive accommodation. He must not take up employment other than that for which he is granted leave to remain. He will be able to change his training employers but only with the permission of the Department of Employment. He will need an entry visa if he is from a visa country.

Q.146 How long can a trainee or someone coming for work experience be allowed to remain?

A.   The period for training is different from that for work experience. Initially he will be given up to three years if he is coming for training and up to 12 months if coming for approved work experience.

If a trainee wishes to extend the period given and applies before the end of the initial period granted then he must show that he entered with a valid Department of Employment work permit or was allowed to remain as a student. A written approval from the Department of Employment will be necessary for an extension and must also show that he continues to meet the requirements stated in the answer to question 145. He may be granted a further period not exceeding three years with the same condition that he may take or change employment only with the permission of the Department of Employment.

If a work experience permit holder wishes to extend his stay and applies before the end of the initial period allocated to him, then he must show that he entered with a valid Department of Employment work experience permit obtained through the employer, or was allowed in as a student, and continues to meet the requirements as stated in the answer to questions 145 and 146. In this case he may be given a further 12 months. The total period he will be allowed will be two years. He too must get the written approval of the Department of Employment for such an extension and may change his employers only with the permission of the Department of Employment.

Q.147 Can either a trainee or work experience permit holder get indefinite leave to remain in the United Kingdom?

A. The rules do not specifically provide for indefinite leave to remain as in the case of work permit holders (as mentioned in the section above under work permits). However it may be argued that, although a permit-free worker, a trainee who has been allowed to stay for three years and has had an extension of his period for a further term exceeding one year may be allowed to remain indefinitely if he has spent a period of four continuous years doing training.

On the other hand a person gaining work experience may not be allowed to remain indefinitely since his total period allowable will not exceed two years and it could not be argued that he can apply, even as a work permit holder, as he could not satisfy the provision that he should have spent a continuous period of four years in Britain.

Q.148 Can the spouse and children of either category be allowed to come in with or join their spouse?

A. The requirements are that, in the case of the spouse, the couple should be married, that the marriage is still subsisting, and that they intend to live together as man and wife. The rule for maintenance remains the same but, as mentioned above, where any dependants are to come in with or join the person here then the rule for accommodation now requires it to be 'exclusive'. The parties should have the intention of leaving the United Kingdom at the end of the period granted them to remain. A valid entry clearance as a spouse is necessary.

With regards to children the general rule applies to the effect that the children should be those of the parents who have been allowed in, that each child should be under 18 years, unmarried, should not have formed a family unit of his own, and should not be leading an independent life. If only one parent is admitted then such children can only join that parent if he has the 'sole responsibility' for the childrens' upbringing or if such parent is the sole surviving parent. In some cases a child will be admitted, even though the above criteria have not been met – for example, where there are serious and compelling family or other reasons which will make refusal of admission of the child undesirable. In such cases suitable arrangements must have been made for his care. Entry clearance is also necessary.

Q.149 Can a visitor apply to vary his category to that of trainee or participant in a work-experience permit scheme?

A.   No. This will not be permitted and may result in curtailment of his leave as a visitor.

Q.150 Can a student apply?

A.   A student is not precluded from applying provided his studies need training or work experience as related and complementary to his qualifications.

WORKING HOLIDAYMAKERS

Q.151 Who is a working holidaymaker?

A.   A working holidaymaker is one who is a Commonwealth citizen, a British dependent territories citizen or British overseas citizen (see question 156 below), aged between 17 and 27 years, or who was so aged when granted leave to enter. He should be unmarried or, if married, then his spouse should also meet all the requirements mentioned herein and they should both intend to take a working holiday together. Where a married spouse applies for this category without the other spouse also applying, it is likely that entry clearance will be refused on the grounds that the marriage is 'on the rocks' and breaking up and that the applicant will not have as strong a reason for returning as before. He must have the means to pay for his return passage if he does not hold a return ticket. There is no harm in having only single tickets in view of the usual practice that a return ticket should be used within one year but if this is the case then he should have the fares for his return guaranteed. The usual requirements that he should be able to adequately accommodate himself (and his spouse and children) without recourse to public funds also apply; he should intend to take up employment which is only incidentally related to a holiday, and he must not engage in business, pursue a career in the United Kingdom, or take up as a professional sportsman or entertainer.

        If he has children, they must not be of the age of five years or above and no child should reach the age of five years before the working holidaymaker reaches the end of his period of leave to remain (which is not more than two years). In effect such a child should not be three years or more at the time of application if the applicant intends to take up the full period allowable. He may take a lesser period if he wishes to remain only until the child is five years old. If his commitments with such children will entail earning a regular income then he will fall short of the requirements.

He must intend to leave the United Kingdom at the end of his period of leave (see questions 48 and 49 above). If he had previously spent a period in the United Kingdom as a working holidaymaker such period will count towards the maximum period he is allowed.

A final requirement is that he must hold a valid entry clearance to enter as a working holidaymaker from his home country, irrespective of the fact that he is a Commonwealth citizen. To get this he must satisfy the entry clearance officer that he can perform all the above requirements.

Q.152 How is the period allowed calculated?

A.   This period is calculated for a period of two years from the first date the applicant was given leave to enter. For instance, if he was given leave from 1 June 1994 and he left the United Kingdom on 30 January 1995 he would have been in the country for eight months. If he wishes to come again he will have to apply well before the end of 30 May 1996. As this is an extension of the first period he will have to satisfy all the requirements mentioned above all over again and get an entry clearance as well. The longer he delays an application for an extension, the shorter will be his stay. The total period of stay that he obtains is two years from the date he was first given leave to enter and the new rules state that, for an extension, he 'would not, as a result of an extension of stay, remain in the United Kingdom as a working holidaymaker to a date beyond 2 years from the date on which he was first given leave to enter the United Kingdom in this capacity.'

He must not have passed the age of 27 when he applies for an extension.

Q.153 Can a working holidaymaker take up employment?

A.   His leave to enter will be subject to a condition restricting the taking up of employment. Only work incidental to a holiday will be allowed and if on applying for an entry clearance the officer has grounds to believe that he will be seeking full employment he will refuse the application (*R v SSHD ex parte Bari* (1987) Imm.A.R. 13). This means that employment must not be the main reason for applying (*SSHD v Grant* (1974) Imm.A.R. 64). He can take up only employment which he is likely to come across during his holiday to supplement his finances. It may be full-time employment for a short period (*re Clive-Lowe* (1992) Imm.A.R. 91) but to be on the side of caution it is advisable to take up only half of the time in full employment. Full-time employment, for this purpose, means working more than 25 hours a week. Part time employment for the full period of his stay may be allowed (*re Clive-Lowe* (1992) Imm.A.R. 91). It is a matter of degree and depends on the facts (*re. Chan* no. 9689). The more onerous the work-time obligations the less is the likelihood that the work will be viewed as incidental. The working holidaymaker will not need a work permit and will not be able to do business, pursue a career or provide services as a professional sportsman or entertainer.

When applying for a visa or entry clearance, or leave to enter, the admission that he could not find a job in his country may militate against him and he may be refused his application.

Q.154   What are the requirements for children?

A.   The rule for working holidaymakers regarding children is not the same as for some other categories where a child should normally be under 18 and satisfy other requirements. In this category, if the working holidaymaker has children they must not be five years or older and a child must not reach the age of five years before the working holidaymaker reaches the end of his period of leave to remain, which is not more than two years. In effect such child should not be three years or more at the time of application if he intends to take up the full period of two years allowable. The child must leave the United Kingdom before reaching the age of five. Perhaps the rationale behind this rule is that children in Britain should start school at five years and if the child of a working holidaymaker stays on he will have to attend school here and that will place a completely different complexion on the status granted. Both parents must have been admitted, or should be being admitted, and the child should be accompanying or joining them. Adequate accommodation and maintenance should be available without recourse to public funds.

If only one parent is admitted then such child/children can only join that parent if such parent has the 'sole responsibility' for the child's/childrens' upbringing or if such parent is the sole surviving parent. In some cases a child will be admitted although the above criteria have not been met – for example, where there are serious and compelling family or other reasons which will make admission of the child desirable. In such cases suitable arrangements must have been made for his care. If the holidaymaker's commitments with any child, or for any reason, will entail earning a regular income, then he will fall short of the entry requirements. A valid entry clearance must first be obtained for each child before he leaves his home country.

The effect of this rule is to further restrict the number who may come in. Unless each child is within the age mentioned above it will mean that such a child will have to be sent back on reaching five years and it is quite likely that one of the parents will have to go too. This, in turn, means that if one parent goes and the other parent stays with another child, such parent must satisfy the 'sole responsibility' rule or 'sole surviving parent' rule. This obviously will not be the case and that will mean both parents leaving or all the children leaving.

Q.155 Will the application be refused if the applicant has settled down in his country before deciding to come to United Kingdom for a working holiday?

A.   Although this requirement has not been clearly defined now, it was part of the old rule that the persons must have been 'coming for an extended holiday before settling down in their own countries'. No mention has been made of this expressly stated old condition in the new rules, nor was any mention made of 'dependants' or 'children'. The new rules do not have any such definite limitations and the old expressly stated condition of coming 'for an extended holiday' has been left out. The new rules state that children under five can accompany their parent subject to what has been said in an earlier question. The information leaflet given out by the Immigration Department states that this is a scheme 'whereby a single person ... comes to the United Kingdom ... before settling down in their own country'. This seems to be at variance with the new rules which allow a parent or parents (where they are married) to be able to come so long as each parent satisfies the requirements. The fact that the parents have been married and the parties have children under five implies some degree of settlement in their country. The case of the one spouse only applying has been mentioned above. In some cases, prior to the new rules, marriage has been held to show that an applicant has settled in his country and therefore does not qualify (*Olaitan Adejumoke v SSHD* (1993) Imm.A.R. 265) because 'before settling' meant 'before becoming established in a more or less permanent abode or way of life' including being in full employment, owning property in his country, or being married. Although there may be some doubts as to this point it is safer to assume that this rule still applies in practice. To avoid all difficulties, take a working holiday before getting married and before 'settling down' in your own country.

Q.156 Will non-Commonwealth citizens be allowed to come as working holidaymakers?

A.   Although the rules state that working holidaymakers should be Commonwealth citizens, the Home Office information leaflet about working holidaymakers states that you must show that you are a Commonwealth citizen, a British dependent territories citizen or British overseas citizen. Any other citizen will be refused and will have no right of appeal. Once again, as the rules take precedence over these 'guidelines' it would appear that only Commonwealth citizens can benefit in this category.

Q.157 Can someone already in the United Kingdom apply to become a holidaymaker?

A.   In view of the new rule requiring that a working holidaymaker should apply for entry clearance 'in this capacity' (in other words as a working holidaymaker) he will be refused leave to remain in the capacity of a working holidaymaker if he entered under a different category and applied whilst in the country to switch to some other category (for example, visitors and students will not be allowed to switch over).

UNITED KINGDOM ANCESTRAL CONNECTIONS

Q.158 Is there any difference if the applicant has ancestral connections with the United Kingdom?

A.   Yes. A Commonwealth citizen only (not any of the other types of citizen) who wishes to come to the United Kingdom on grounds of ancestral connections can do so if he applies when he is 17 years old or over (*re Leahy* no. 7981). Ancestral connections mean that the applicant has one of his grandparents born in the United Kingdom and islands. He should be able to work (not as a working holidaymaker but generally) and be seeking employment in the United Kingdom. He does not need a work permit. He must also be able to accommodate and maintain himself and any dependants adequately without recourse to public funds. He must apply abroad for an entry clearance in this capacity before coming and must show evidence of meeting all the requirements mentioned. It may, however, be possible to switch in the United Kingdom to this category if all the requirements are present. Ancestral connection by a Commonwealth citizen does not apply to an illegitimate child claiming through paternal grandparents. The applicant must produce evidence of his grandparent's birth certificate, his parent's birth certificate, and his own birth certificate (all documents must be originals).

Q.159 What countries are referred to as the United Kingdom and islands?

A.   The United Kingdom and islands for this purpose are comprised of England, Wales, Scotland, Northern Ireland and the Isle of Man and the Channel Islands. In addition, what is now the Republic of Ireland will be considered if the grandparent was born there before 31 March 1922.

Q.160 How long will someone with ancestral connections be granted leave to stay?

A.   He will be granted leave to stay for a period up to, but not exceeding four years. After this period he can obtain indefinite leave to remain if he applies for such leave before the end of the four years. He must have spent a continuous period of the four years of his leave in the United Kingdom in employment and must have satisfied all the other requirements.

Q.161. Can such a person bring his spouse and children with him or to join him?

A.   Yes. He must actually be married to the spouse and they must intend to live together as man and wife. He must satisfy the requirements for accommodation and maintenance as mentioned and the accommodation must be exclusively for their use. The spouse will be allowed for the same period as the applicant and must show her intention of leaving at the end of such period granted. An entry clearance will be necessary before the spouse can accompany or join the applicant. Where indefinite leave to remain is applied for by the spouse with such United Kingdom ancestral connection, he can also apply for his spouse to remain indefinitely.

His children can also accompany or join him if such children are under 18 years. Both parents must have been admitted or be in the process of being admitted and the child/children must be accompanying or joining them and adequate accommodation and maintenance must be available without recourse to public funds.

If only one parent is admitted then such a child/children can only join that parent if he has the 'sole responsibility' for the child/childrens' upbringing or if such parent is the sole surviving parent. In some cases a child will be admitted even though the above criteria have not been met − for example, where there are serious and compelling family or other reasons which will make admission of the child desirable. In such cases suitable arrangements must have been made for his care.

Q.162 Can someone with United Kingdom ancestry who entered the United Kingdom in any other capacity be able to remain in the United Kingdom in this capacity?

A.   Yes. Anyone who qualifies as having United Kingdom ancestry as defined above and satisfies all the requirements as mentioned in the answer to question 159 will be able to seek leave to remain in the United Kingdom in this capacity irrespective of the category he first entered under.

AU PAIRS

Q.163 Who can become an au pair?

A.   Citizens, male or female, of the following countries are eligible to participate under the au pair scheme:

Andora, Bosnia-Herzegovina, Croatia, Cyprus, Czech Republic, the Faroes, Greenland, Hungary, Liechtenstein*, Macedonia, Malta, Monaco, San Marino, Slovak Republic, Slovenia, Switzerland, Turkey.

Citizens of the European Economic Area Agreement no longer need leave to enter or remain in the United Kingdom (this came into force in January 1994).

* Liechtenstein will soon be deleted from this list when it endorses the European Economic Area agreement. This means that its citizens will not need to qualify under the rules to enter and remain and can enter and remain to work or study without formalities.

Help for 'au pairs' to find host families can be arranged.

Q.164 What are the requirements to be satisfied?

A.   Such a person must be between the age of 17 and 27. If she is under the age of 27 when she was first granted leave to enter but has exceeded that age she may be allowed to remain and continue the full period allowable to 'au pairs'.

She must come to the United Kingdom with the intention of learning the English language and must live for a time with an English speaking family and must have appropriate opportunities for studies. Such applicant must also help in the home for a period of a maximum of five hours per day for which she must receive a reasonable allowance (between £20–30 per week) as pocket money. Two free days per week must be allowed to her and she must be provided with her own room in the family household. The applicant must be single and without dependants and must not intend to stay in the United Kingdom beyond the two years allowable as an au pair. She must show the immigration officer that arrangements have already been made with an English-speaking family and that all the requirements have been approved by the family, including the allowance to be made to her. Each period applied for can be less than two years but if this is the case then any application for an extension may be granted but the total period allowed will not exceed two years.

Q.165 How is the period allowable calculated?

A. If the applicant has previously spent time in the United Kingdom as an au pair then the period of two years is calculated from the first date she was given leave to enter the country. For instance, if she was first given leave on 1 July 1994 and she left United Kingdom on 30 January 1995 she would have been in the country for seven months. If she wishes to come again she will have to apply well before the end of 30 June 1996 when her two years (from 1 July 1994) would have expired. As this extension will be calculated from the first period (1 July 1994) she will only get an extension (or a further extension) lasting up to 30 June 1996. The longer she delays an application for an extension whilst away from the United Kingdom, the shorter will be her stay. She will have to satisfy all the requirements mentioned above all over again.

Q.166 Do all au pairs need entry clearance?

A. The new rules do not make such a requirement but they state that it is advisable for non-visa nationals wishing to ascertain in advance whether their placements are likely to meet the requirements to apply for entry clearance (see the answers to question 6 *et seq*. in Chapter 1 for those countries whose nationals are visa-nationals). This implies that a visa national should obtain a visa or an entry clearance beforehand. Visa nationals in this category are those of Bosnia-Herzegovina, Macedonia, and Turkey. It is advisable for the au pair to obtain a letter from the family that she is coming to stay with explaining the arrangements and the duties that she will be expected to carry out.

Q.167 Can an au pair seek employment whilst remaining here as such?

A. No. Au pairs are only allowed to do light household work and take care of any children. This arrangement is not considered as employment and she is not considered as a domestic servant. Her passport will be stamped with a prohibition on employment except as an au pair. 'Au pairing' must be shown to be the sole intention and au pairs must not seek other full time employment (*Ramjane v Chief Immig. Officer, Heathrow Airport* (1973) Imm.A.R. 84).

Q.168 Can someone who entered in another category but who would otherwise have satisfied the rules change to become an au pair?

A.   If a person has not been granted leave to enter as an au pair she will be refused an extension if she applies to remain as au pair. She must leave the United Kingdom and re-apply to enter as such.

Q.169 Can an au pair move from one family to another?

A.   Yes, she may change families so long as she continues to meet all the requirements for an au pair. Such changes will not add to the total period for which she is entitled to remain in the country. All previous periods as an au pair will be tallied.

SEASONAL AGRICULTURAL WORKERS

Q.170 Who is classified as a seasonal agricultural worker?

A.   This category does not need a work permit. Certain farmers in the United Kingdom operate a scheme whereby young agricultural workers are employed seasonally in their farms for short periods. Such schemes are approved by the Secretary of State beforehand. An applicant who wishes to enter the United Kingdom under such a scheme should be one who is in full-time education in his country and is aged between 18 and 25 years. This age limitation may be overlooked if he is returning for another season at the agricultural camp at the request of the farmer. He must apply for and obtain a Home Office work card issued by the operator of the approved scheme. His intention must not be to take up employment other than that of a seasonal agricultural worker (mainly for harvesting) for a specific period and he must intend to return home at the end of his period of leave. He will not need entry clearance if he is not a visa-national. As accommodation and some remuneration is part of the scheme, such students who come to work in agricultural farms do not have to satisfy the usual requirements mentioned for students or other workers coming to study or work in the United Kingdom.

Q.171 How long can such a person be allowed to stay?

A. The leave to remain in the United Kingdom will be for a period not exceeding three months. This period, however, should not extend beyond 30 November of the year of his entry. This means that if he entered at any time after 1 September (say on 27 September) his stay will only last until 30 November and he would have lost 27 days which he could have stayed if he had entered on 1 September. If he enters before 1 September then he can only stay for 3 months from the date of such entry.

Q.172 Can this period be extended?

A. If such a student entered with a valid work card as mentioned above, and satisfies the immigration officer that he intends to return at the end of the period and does not intend to take other employment, then provided that there is further farm work available under the scheme he may be granted an extension (if the application is made before the expiry date of his leave). Such extension will not exceed six months in total and the same rule applies that he will not be allowed to remain beyond 30 November. This means that any extension over the previous three months will not necessarily be for a further three months if this further period will mean staying beyond 30 November.

Q.173 Can he bring his wife and dependants with him?

A. The rules do not provide for this and unless the wife is herself a student aged 17–25 and has applied in her own right to enter under the scheme then she or any dependants will be refused entry.

TEACHERS AND LANGUAGE ASSISTANTS

Q.174 What are the requirements to be satisfied by teachers and language assistants?

A. Entry must be under an exchange scheme that has been approved by the Education Department or one which is administered by the Central Bureau for Educational Visits and Exchanges, or by the League for Exchange of Commonwealth Teachers. The applicant must be coming to an educational establishment in the United Kingdom under one of those schemes. His intention must be to work only within the approved scheme and not to seek employment. He must also intend to leave the United Kingdom immediately when his exchange period runs out. He must be able to accommodate and to maintain himself and any dependants without recourse to public funds. Before leaving he must obtain an entry clearance for this category.

Q.175   How long will he be allowed to remain in the United Kingdom?

A.   The initial period will be 12 months. If he wishes to extend this period he should, before the end of the initial period, apply for such an extension. Provided he had a valid entry clearance at the start, and is still engaged in the employment, and his services are certified by the employers as still being required, and he also continues to satisfy the requirements mentioned in the answer to question 174 above, he may be given another 12 months' leave to remain, making the maximum of two years that he can stay.

Q.176   Can he bring his spouse with him or to join him?

A.   Yes. They must actually be married and intend to live together during their stay and the marriage must be subsisting. Adequate accommodation and maintenance must be available without recourse to public funds. The accommodation must be exclusively for their use. A shared kitchen, bathroom and so forth, in a shared house with other tenants will lead to the accommodation failing to qualify as 'exclusive', although indications are that this requirement may be relaxed where there is at least a bedroom exclusively for the couple's use. The applicant's intention and that of his spouse must be to leave the United Kingdom at the end of the period of their leave to stay. The spouse will need an entry clearance for this category. If the spouse came in under any other category and wishes to remain as spouse for the extended period of the applicant's stay she will be refused.

Q.177   Can the children be allowed to come with or join the parents?

A.   If the child is that of the parent who is coming (or who has already entered) as a teacher or language assistant, and the child is under 18 years and single, has not set up a separate family unit of his own and can be accommodated (in accommodation as mentioned before), and maintained without recourse to public funds, then he will be allowed in if he also shows an intention not to remain after his leave has expired and both parents are in the United Kingdom. He must obtain an entry clearance before coming. If only one parent is admitted then such child can only join that parent if the parent has the 'sole responsibility' for the child's upbringing, or if such parent is the sole surviving parent. In some cases a child will be admitted although the above criteria have not been met – for example, where there are serious and compelling family or other reasons which will make refusal of the child undesirable. In such cases suitable arrangements must have been made for his care.

OVERSEAS GOVERNMENT EMPLOYEES

Q.178 Who is an overseas government employee?

A. Anyone coming for employment by an overseas government, or by the United Nations, or any other international organisation of which the United Kingdom is a member. Such a person will not be coming to work in the Embassy or High Commission of his country in the United Kingdom and is considered as a permit-free worker.

Q.179 What are the requirements to be satisfied?

A. He must intend to work full time for the government or the organisation employing him and not to take up employment elsewhere. He must also be able to accommodate and maintain himself and any dependants without recourse to public funds. He must obtain an entry clearance for this purpose and evidence of employment by the government or organisation should be provided.

Q.180 How long can such an employee be given to remain in the United Kingdom?

A. The initial period will be up to 12 months and if he wishes to extend this period then he and his employers must show that he was first given leave to enter as an employee of the overseas government or of the United Nations or other organisation of which the United Kingdom is a member. He must still be in this employment and still be required at the time of the application to continue in the employment. It must also be shown that he continues to accommodate and maintain himself and any dependants as mentioned above. The intention of staying in the same employment for the same employer must also be indicated. If the immigration authorities are satisfied that all these requirements will be met and the application has been made before the end of the period of 12 months initially granted then his stay may be extended for a further term of up to three years. Thereafter it is possible for him to obtain indefinite leave to remain provided an application is made before the end of the extended period and he continues to satisfy all the requirements and has been in the United Kingdom for a continuous period of four years. (This continuous period has been explained before).

Q.181 Can his spouse or children come in with him or join him?

A.   Yes. With regard to a spouse, they must be married, the marriage must still be subsisting, and the couple must intend to live together as man and wife during their stay in the Britain. There must be adequate accommodation and maintenance for the family without recourse to public funds and, in these circumstances, the accommodation must be exclusively for their own use (but see question 176 above). The parties must not intend to remain beyond the period granted them. An entry clearance must be obtained by the spouse and children.

The children must be under 18 and single, and must not have formed separate family units or be living independently. Both parents must have been admitted into the United Kingdom or must be admitted at the same time. If only one parent has been admitted then such children must be the 'sole responsibility' of the parent admitted or he must be the sole surviving parent responsible for their upbringing, or there must be a serious and compelling reason that will make excluding such children undesirable. If this last case is the reason for admission, suitable arrangements for the childrens' care must have been made before applying for an entry clearance for them.

The period granted to the spouse and children will be the same period granted to the applicant spouse and the parents, including extension and indefinite leave to remain.

PRIVATE SERVANTS IN DIPLOMATIC HOUSEHOLDS

Q.182 What are the requirements for a private servant in a diplomatic household to enter?

A.   He should be 18 years or over and should be entering as a private servant of an employer who is a member of staff of a diplomatic or consular mission. The employer should be one who either enjoys diplomatic immunity and other privileges as provided in the Convention covering such persons (the Vienna Convention on Diplomatic and Consular Relations) or a member of the family of such a person who forms part of the same household: The servant's intention is to work full time in the employment of his employer and not to take up employment in any other way. He should be able to accommodate and maintain himself and his dependants adequately without recourse to public funds. He must apply for an entry clearance before coming to the United Kingdom. The servant's capacity may be that of a maid or driver or nanny or any such person usually found in a household.

Q.183 How long can such a servant be allowed to work in the United Kingdom?

A.   He may be allowed up to 12 months initially if he obtains an entry clearance for this purpose. If he wishes to extend this period he must make an application before the end of the initial period granted and he should show that he entered as such a servant and provide a certificate from his employer to prove that he is still in his employment and is still needed for the position as a servant in his household. The other requirements for extension are that provision for accommodation and maintenance must be shown to be adequate and no recourse to public funds must have been taken. When these things have been proved he may then have his period of stay extended up to a further 12 months.

It is now possible, under the new rules, for such applicants to obtain indefinite leave to remain. This was not possible before 1 October 1994. If the servant is granted further extensions amounting to four years, and has been in the United Kingdom continuously for that period in the same employment, and is certified as still being required by his employer for the work he entered to do originally then he may be granted indefinite leave to remain. It must, however, be said that as such diplomats or family members employing such servants are usually in the United Kingdom for less than four years then it may not be possible for the servant to satisfy the requirements for indefinite leave. Where a new employer wishes to retain the services of the servant who came in through a different employer a new application may be required and a new entry clearance from abroad may be needed. This will then place the servant in the same position of not being able to satisfy the requirements. In short it may not be likely for such a servant to get indefinite leave to remain unless the employer has been in the United Kingdom for a period of four years or more and the servant has been with him for the required four years.

Q.184 Can a servant in a diplomatic household bring in his spouse and children?

A.   Yes. The same requirements apply as mentioned in the answer to question 182 above (spouses and children of overseas government employees).

Q.185 What will be the position if a servant in employment in a diplomatic household finds another job with another employer who is not a diplomat?

A.   The most likely result will be that the servant will have to make an application for his stay to be varied to that category and the employer will have to obtain a work permit for him, but this is likely to be refused and the worker will have to leave the country and start all over again unless the employer can show that the worker has exceptional skills in his work and that these skills are not easily available in the United Kingdom.

DOMESTIC SERVANTS (NOT DIPLOMATIC EMPLOYEES)

Q.186 Can a domestic servant be allowed into the United Kingdom if not coming to work for a diplomat or someone in a consular position or a member of their family?

A.   There are no provisions in the rules for such a servant to come in. Where there are no provisions it means that any entry is solely at the discretion of the Secretary of State outside the rules. This concession is not usually granted except to rich or expatriate families who wish to continue to employ their domestic servants from overseas. It is not granted to employers already established in the United Kingdom who wish to recruit new domestic staff from overseas.

The concession, now formally acknowledged, provides that, from 1991, if the employer is only coming for a visit, such servants must be 18 years or over (as from December 1994) and must have been in the employment of the employer for 12 months or more overseas. If the employer is coming for any other purpose the servant must have been in employment for at least 24 months. An entry clearance will be needed before coming and during the interview a check will be made to see if the employee knows that he is coming as an employee, the hours of work he will be doing each day, and that he wants to come to the United Kingdom. An entry clearance or visa to enter as a domestic servant is not a work permit. All interviews with the servant will be made conducted separately from those with the employer. The servant will be prohibited from working for any other employer, and the employer will be required to give a written guarantee that adequate provision will be made for the maintenance and accommodation of the employee, and this must include a separate bedroom.

Domestic service for only two mornings a week will not be sufficient to allow a servant to qualify as a domestic servant. A document outlining the terms and conditions is given to the employee on application for entry clearance to come to Britain and it also explains his rights and the position on entry, and addresses to go to for help or advice. It is always advisable for employees to keep their passports in a safe place where they can easily get at them – preferably not with their employers.

Q.187 How long can such a servant be allowed to remain?

A.   The period granted will be in line with that granted to the employer. Thus a visiting employer will get a maximum of six months and so will the employee. There can be no extension beyond the six months. Where the employer is coming to reside in the United Kingdom the employee's passport will be stamped with leave to remain with a prohibition of taking employment other than with the employer who brought him in. Normally the period will be 12 months, renewable after that period on application made before the initial period is due to expire. The employee has no independent legal status and his stay is dependent on the employer. If he is sacked he can stay in the United Kingdom, if he can support himself, until the time granted for him to stay expires. He will be deported when the period granted him expires if he is still here. The servant may have certain employment rights such as notice of dismissal, or a claim for unfair dismissal (if he has grounds), or for redundancy payment, depending on the period served. After four years in continuous service with the same employer indefinite leave may be granted at the discretion of the Home Office and 'outside the rules'.

Q.188 Can a domestic servant change his employers?

A.   The answer is no. Any application to change will be at the discretion of the Home Office and it is unlikely that it will be granted except under exceptional circumstances. If the reason for wanting to change is cruel treatment (for example assault by the employer) it is possible for criminal charges to be brought against the employer, but this does not give a right to change employer. The servant can, after being in the United Kingdom for four years, apply for indefinite leave to remain and, if this is granted, he will then not be subject to any work restrictions and may take up employment of any kind. The only instance where the servant can stay and work when his employer leaves is where the employer's immediate family are also visiting but staying on when the employer on a visit leaves before the six month period granted as a visitor. The employee will have to leave before the six month period stamped on his passport expires.

Q.189 Does a servant have to travel with his master every time he travels out of the United Kingdom on short visits?

A.   No. If the employer is living in Britain, for as long as he is lawfully based here and intends to return, the servant does not need to leave. If the employer leaves permanently it is likely that the servant will also leave. If the servant stays he cannot work for another employer and must leave before the expiry of the six months granted him where the employer entered as a visitor and both he and the servant had only six months leave or, alternatively, at the end of the 12 months granted where his employer entered for a longer period and not as a visitor.

Q.190 What if he marries in the United Kingdom to a British citizen?

A.   The same rule will apply as given in the answer to question 52 above.

MINISTERS OF RELIGION, MISSIONARIES, MEMBERS OF RELIGIOUS ORDERS

Q.191 Who are considered as ministers of religion?

A.   A 'functionary whose main regular duties comprise the leading of a congregation in performing the rites and rituals of the faith and in preaching the essentials of the creed.'

Q.192 Who are considered as missionaries?

A.   A missionary is 'a person who is directly engaged in spreading a religious doctrine and whose work is not administrative or clerical.'

Q.193 Who are considered as members of a religious order?

A.   They are those who wish to enter into the United Kingdom to live in a community run by that order (for example, to live in a monastery or a nunnery) and be a part of its life or to teach in schools run by such orders.

Q.194 Are the entry requirements the same for each or are there different requirements?

A.   There are some differences for each category but a few of the other requirements are common.

Q.195 What are the requirements for a minister of religion to enter the United Kingdom as such?

A.   He must be a religious functionary who wishes to enter Britain to lead a congregation in performing the rites and preaching the tenets of his creed. He must obtain a visa or entry clearance to enter Britain as a minister of religion and not as a visitor. He will have to show the need for his work in the United Kingdom and provide details of his employment.

He could only enter as a visitor for the purpose of a job interview or for a short tour and will have to change his entry category if he is appointed as leader of his congregation. It may be possible to change from a visitor to a minister of religion but this change will have to be made from outside the United Kingdom unless, of course, the Home Office accepts an application from within the United Kingdom as a concession.

The minister of religion must have been working as such for at least a year before the application. If his religion prescribes ordination in order for him to perform his duties then he must have had a year's full-time training or two years' part-time training before such ordination.

He must intend to work as a full-time minister of religion and must not take up employment except as such, must have adequate maintenance and accommodation for himself and any dependants without recourse to public funds.

Q.196 What are the requirements for a missionary to enter as such?

A.   He must be trained as a missionary or have worked as a missionary and is being sent to the United Kingdom by his organisation overseas. The other requirements are the same as for a minister of religion – he must intend to work as a full-time missionary and not have an intention of taking up employment except as such, and he must be able to adequately accommodate and maintain himself and any dependants without recourse to public funds. He must obtain an entry clearance before coming to the United Kingdom for this purpose and will have to show full details of the posting and the need for his employment here.

Q.197 What are the requirements for entry as a member of a religious order?

A.   The applicant must be coming to live in a community maintained by the religious order to which he belongs. If he intends to teach the tenets of his religious order he must only do so in an establishment maintained by his order. The other requirements for the other categories also apply. He must intend to work as a full-time member of his religious order, and not have an intention of taking up employment except as such. If he does teach in schools not within the order, the school must obtain a work permit for him. He must show that he can adequately accommodate and maintain himself and any dependants without recourse to public funds; he will normally be maintained and housed by the religious order. He must obtain an entry clearance before coming to the United Kingdom for this purpose.

Q.198 How long can each of these categories remain in the United Kingdom?

A.   The initial period will not exceed 12 months. If the applicant intends to extend the initial period granted he must apply before the expiry of this period and, provided he can satisfy the immigration authorities that he entered with a valid entry clearance (or visa) for the purpose it was granted and is still engaged in the same employment and he is certified by the leaders of his congregation (minister of religion) or his employers (missionary) or the head of his religious order as still being required for the employment, and continues to satisfy the various requirements for his type of work including accommodation and maintenance as mentioned above, he may be granted a further period of three years. If he wishes to apply for indefinite leave to remain in the United Kingdom and applies before the end of the further term given him then he may be able to obtain this if he has spent a continuous period of four years in the United Kingdom in the same capacity as he first entered and continues to satisfy all the requirements for his category and is still required by the leaders of his congregation or employer or religious order.

Q.199 Can any of the above categories have his spouse and children accompany or join him?

A.   Yes. He must actually be married to the spouse, and they must intend to live together as man and wife. He must satisfy the requirements for accommodation and maintenance as mentioned and the accommodation must be exclusively for their use. (This requirement may be satisfied if there is a bedroom exclusively for their use.) The spouse will be allowed for the same period as the applicant and must show her intention of leaving at the end of the period granted. An entry clearance will be necessary before the spouse can accompany or join the applicant. Where an extension, including indefinite leave to remain, is applied for, the spouse (minister, missionary or member of a religious order) can also apply for his spouse and children to remain.

His children can also accompany or join him if such children are under 18 years. Both parents must have been admitted or must be in the process of being admitted, the children must be accompanying or joining them, and adequate accommodation and maintenance must be available without recourse to public funds.

If only one parent is admitted then such children can only join that parent if he has the 'sole responsibility' for the childrens' upbringing or if such parent is the sole surviving parent. In some cases a child will be admitted even though the above criteria have not been met – for example, where there are serious and compelling family or other reasons which will make admission of the child desirable. In such cases suitable arrangements must have been made for his care.

Q.200 Can a minister of religion also teach as a member of a religious order?

A.   No. these are two distinct and full-time activities. The rules as drafted seem to distinguish between two 'distinct and mutually exclusive activities' and doing both will make each a part-time occupation and thus will not fulfil the requirements for either. (*Ajoy Shankar Chowdhury v ECO, Calcutta*) He can teach the faith as a minister of religion but this must be his full time occupation.

Q.201 Can a minister of religion change his employment?

A.   This may be allowed only if the change is of employer and the permission of the immigration authorities is required. He will still have to satisfy all the requirements as before. If he wishes to change his type of employment from that of minister of religion to something different this will not be allowed.

Chapter 7

Entry for other purposes

RETIRED PERSONS OF INDEPENDENT MEANS

Q.202 Who is considered as a person of independent means?

A.   He must be 60 years of age or over, retired, and in possession of a disposable income in the United Kingdom of at least £25 000 per annum. He must intend to make the United Kingdom his main home and must have close connections with the country (see also question 41).

Q.203 What are the requirements for such a person to come to the United Kingdom?

A.   He must be 60 or over and have an income in the United Kingdom of £25 000 per annum of his own money, under his control and freely disposable by him (see *ex parte Kok Meng Chiew* (1981) Imm.A.R. 102), he must have close connections with the United Kingdom (see *SSHD v Raquel Teresa Rohr* (1983) Imm.A.R. 95) and the intention of making the United Kingdom his main home. There is no longer the former requirement that this is 'in the general interest of the United Kingdom' (as is the case for those coming for self-employment). Consideration may be given to applicants who have assets of over half a million pounds where there is no close connection with the United Kingdom.

The applicant must also be able to accommodate and maintain himself and any of his dependants indefinitely from his own finances without any help from anyone else. He must be able to undertake all these financial obligations without taking any employment and without recourse to public funds. In the new rules the requirement is for a minimum sum of £25 000 a year as income with no figure fixed as a minimum sum to be owned (as was previously the case). This makes the financial requirements more onerous. To have an income of £25 000 per year means an investment of about half a million pounds (at the time of writing). The Home Office may consider an income slightly less than the obligatory one as a concession.

He must obtain an entry clearance (or visa) from whichever country he is coming from for the particular purpose of coming to the United Kingdom to settle as a retired person of independent means.

Q.204 How long will such a person be allowed in the United Kingdom?

A.   He will be granted a period of anything up to but not exceeding four years initially. This period will be subject to a condition prohibiting employment. If he was granted less than four years he can apply before the end of the period granted for an extension of that period. If he shows that he continues to satisfy all the requirements and that he has made the United Kingdom his main home, his period may be extended to the full four years but not more. The period of four years can be aggregated. This means any period of presence in the United Kingdom with breaks in between will be totalled and his extension will be up to the period making up the four years. (This is different from some other categories we have seen, such as the au pair category, where the total period allowable is from the date of granting entry up to the end of the period allowable and any break in between is counted in the period allowable.)

Q.205 Can a spouse or children accompany or join the person applying to enter as a person of independent means?

A.   Yes. The same conditions apply as mentioned in previous answers. He must actually be married to the spouse and they must intend to live together as man and wife. He must satisfy the requirements for accommodation and maintenance as mentioned, and the accommodation must be exclusively for the couple's use (see above on this). The spouse will be allowed to stay for the same period as the applicant and must show her intention of leaving at the end of such period granted. An entry clearance will be necessary before the spouse can accompany or join the applicant. Where an extension, including indefinite leave to remain, is applied for, the spouse and children will be given the same period as the applicant. His children can also accompany or join him if such children are under 18 years. Both parents must have been admitted or be in the process of admission, the children must be accompanying or joining them, and adequate accommodation and maintenance must be available without recourse to public funds. If only one parent is admitted then such children can only join that parent if he has the 'sole responsibility' for the childrens' upbringing or if such parent is the sole surviving parent.

In some cases a child will be admitted although the above criteria have not been met – for instance, where there are serious and compelling family or other reasons which will make admission of the child desirable. In such cases suitable arrangements must be made for his care.

Q.206 Can such a person obtain indefinite leave to remain?

A.   As indicated above he must intend to make the United Kingdom his main home. This means settlement, and so he will be granted a period not exceeding four years initially, or four years aggregated. Before the end of the last period granted, making up the four years, he may apply for indefinite leave to remain provided he continues to show that he has been satisfying all the requirements and has stayed in the United Kingdom for a continuous period of four years (see above for 'continuous period'). If applying for his spouse and dependants for indefinite leave to remain, he must do so at the same time as he applies for himself.

Q.207 Can the spouse or children take employment?

A.   For the period that they are in the United Kingdom under limited leave to remain – in other words, if they have not applied for indefinite leave to remain after four years' stay – they will be prohibited from working. After the indefinite leave to remain has been granted all such prohibition will be removed.

ACCESS TO A CHILD RESIDENT IN THE UNITED KINGDOM

Q.208 Who has the right to enter the United Kingdom in order to exercise right of access to his child?

A.   A parent living abroad who has such a right is one who has been granted the right of access to his child resident in the United Kingdom by a court in the United Kingdom. The parent must be either divorced or legally separated from his wife.

Q.209 What are the requirements for such entry?

A.   The applicant will need an entry clearance specifically for this purpose and he should apply in his country for this clearance. The parent must show the court order granting him leave to access to his child, and show that he is divorced or legally separated from his wife. He must be able to meet the cost of his return journey (a return ticket will be helpful), and (as usual with most other categories) must prove that he is able to adequately accommodate and maintain himself and any dependants coming with him for such access visit without recourse to public funds and without taking up employment. In this category adequate accommodation and maintenance can be provided by friends or relatives. Whilst in the United Kingdom he must not have any intention of taking employment, nor provide services (including selling of goods) directly to the public. A further intention must be shown of leaving the United Kingdom at the end of the period granted him.

Q.210 How long will such leave be?

A. Such leave (with a prohibition on employment) will not be for more than 12 months.

Q.211 Can he extend this period?

A. The rules do not provide for an extension and so any such request will be at the discretion of the Secretary of State and it is unlikely to be granted except in serious exceptional circumstances.

Q.212 How often can such a visit take place?

A. This will depend on the court order. If it grants a visit once a year then he will be entitled to an access visit once a year. In such a case it is unlikely that 12 months will be granted unless the order provides such a period for the visit, which is also unlikely. The parent has to leave at the end of the period granted by the immigration authorities and must apply again for the next visit, depending on the terms granted by the order.

Q.213 What is meant by the requirement that the parent must be divorced or legally separated from his wife?

A. This means divorced or legally separated from the other parent of the child (through a court process). If such a parent has remarried then he can still obtain access to the child in the United Kingdom and his current spouse and children may be able to accompany him to the United Kingdom (as his dependants) for his access visit.

DIPLOMATS

Q.214 Who are diplomats?

A.   These are people employed by their countries to represent them
abroad. Under international law they are considered to be working in
the country employing them and as such do not need a work permit.
They are dealt with by the Foreign and Commonwealth Office. The
countries concerned send lists of those in their diplomatic service to
this office. They are given entry clearance upon request from their
home governments but such clearance takes the form of a stamp to
show that they are not subject to immigration control. The exemption
continues until it is cancelled by the Home Office after it has been
notified that the diplomatic person is no longer employed by his
country. He then has 28 days grace to remain, within which period he
may make an application to remain for longer than this period in
another category.

It does not matter how long a diplomat has been in the Britain in
that capacity, his stay cannot qualify him for settlement. Someone
already in the Britain may not apply to change into an employee in the
diplomatic service whilst he is still in the United Kingdom.

Q.215 What of the spouses of those in the diplomatic service?

A.   They too are exempt from immigration control and the immigration
authorities cannot deprive them of exemption by refusing leave to
enter and requiring an entry clearance (*Immigration Officer, Heathrow
v Abd Halim bin Abd Rahman* IAT (April 1994 no. TH/61484/92).
Members of the family who form part of the household, and persons
otherwise entitled to immunity from jurisdiction as is conferred by the
Diplomatic Privileges Act 1964, are free from control. This Act divides
members of the diplomatic missions into three categories:

   (i) members of the diplomatic staff and their families granted full
        personal immunity from both civil and criminal liabilities
        (except in some limited instances);

   (ii) members of the administrative and technical staff given full
        immunity in respect of their official acts but have civil but not
        criminal liability for acts done outside their official duties;

   (iii) members of the domestic service staff who have full immunity
        for their official acts but attract civil and criminal liabilities for
        acts carried out outside their official course of duty.

Q.216 Are those in employment in diplomatic missions subject to immigration control?

A.   Normally the answer is 'no'. If, however, the person was employed locally in the United Kingdom then he is not considered outside immigration control. If he left to come to the United Kingdom and was offered the post, he is not exempt. If, on the other hand, the post was offered to him abroad and he entered to take up such a post he is covered by the Diplomatic Privileges Act 1964 and is exempt.

EUROPEAN UNION NATIONALS

Q.217 Which countries make up the European Union?

A.   Belgium, Denmark, France, Germany, Greece, Ireland, Italy, Luxembourg, Netherlands, Portugal, Spain, the United Kingdom, Austria, Finland, Iceland, Norway, Sweden have now joined and Liechtenstein has joined but has yet to ratify the agreement.

Q.218 Can any EU national enter the United Kingdom without an entry permit?

A.   The 1988 Immigration Act provides that an EU national does not need leave to enter or remain here if he is entering by an enforceable Union right. The immigration (European Economic Area) order 1994 states that EU nationals may enter on production of a national identity card or passport issued by another EU country.

Under this Order he must be entering as self-employed or seeking employment. The right of an EU citizen to reside in Britain has an economic basis. He does not have an unqualified right of residence. He must be employed or seeking employment with a very good chance of finding it. Whilst seeking employment in the United Kingdom he is entitled to benefits such as income support but, after a while, if he cannot obtain employment and is claiming benefits, he can be sent away for becoming a burden on the State (*R v SSHD ex parte Vitale* TLR 25 January 1996 overturning a previous ruling in *ex parte Antonissen*).

A member of such a person's family may also be admitted if he can produce evidence that he is a family member. If such a family member is not a national of the EU then if he is a visa national, he must have a 'family residence permit' before entering. A 'family permit' means an entry clearance issued (free) to a member of the EU person's family who is himself not an EU national and who is a visa national or is one coming to join a qualified EU national. Where such a family member arrives in the United Kingdom without a permit it is not likely that such a person will be turned away if evidence is available of the family relationship with the EU national. EU nationals will be issued with a five-year residence permit if they are workers, self-employed, a provider of services, a recipient of services, a self-sufficient person, a retired person, a self-employed person who has ceased economic activities in the United Kingdom, or a student. These categories are described as 'qualified persons'. Their families may also join them if they have an EU family permit. Certain exceptions based on public policy, public security, or public health may exclude some individuals.

Where a British citizen wishes to bring a non-British European national spouse to Britain under the European Union Agreement the position taken by Britain is that such a spouse must satisfy British rules for spouses to enter rather than the less rigorous requirements of the European directive even though this was tested in the case of *Surrinder Singh* (1992) 3 CMLR 358 which ruled against the British stand. It seems that a British citizen coming to Britain with a spouse is not considered as a European Union national.

Q.219   Who are considered as family members in such cases?

A.   For those 'qualified persons' mentioned above, except students, family consists of the spouse, children up to the age of 21 or older if they are still dependent, dependent parents, grandparents, and great grand-parents. In the case of students, only spouses and dependent children are regarded as family members.

Spouses do not include, for the purposes of United Kingdom immigration, a party to a 'marriage of convenience'. This has been defined as meaning a marriage entered into solely for immigration purposes where neither partner has the intention of living permanently together genuinely as man and wife. Although this is akin to the primary purpose rule, primary purpose tests do not apply to EU marriage cases.

Q.220   Can an EU national remain indefinitely in the United Kingdom?

A.   The rules provide for settlement of EU nationals and their families. Those issued with residence permits for five years who have remained for four years (in accordance with the EU order) and continue to do so may apply for indefinite leave to remain.

A self-employed person who has a right to reside in the United Kingdom by virtue of having ceased economic activities in the United Kingdom may obtain indefinite leave to remain, as well as any family member. An EU national who has been continuously resident in the United Kingdom for three or more years and has been in employment in the last 12 months in any of the EU states, and has reached retirement age in any of the states he was working in, or where he has ceased employment because of incapacity due to accident at work or to an occupational disease which entitles him to a disability pension, or has been continuously resident in the United Kingdom for at least two years and has ceased employment due to permanent disability, may apply for such leave. Members of the families of such EU nationals as mentioned above may also be allowed indefinite leave to remain, as may the member of the family of an EU national who dies during his working life after being in the United Kingdom for two years continuously if such death results from accident at work or from occupational disease.

Chapter 8

Settlement

RIGHT OF ABODE

Q.221 Who has the right of abode in the United Kingdom?

A.   Under the Immigration Act 1971 as amended by the British Nationality Act 1981:

(1) anyone who is a British citizen; or

(2) a Commonwealth citizen who before 1 January 1983 (the commencement date of the British Nationality Act 1981) had the right of abode in the United Kingdom (that is, persons settled in the United Kingdom and islands without being subject to immigration control and who have not ceased to be Commonwealth citizens in the meantime).

The 1981 British Nationality Act is now the main Act which defines nationality and the right of abode. It amended the Immigration Act 1971. A woman who marries a British citizen after 1 January 1983 does not thereby acquire a right of abode and requires an entry clearance (*Brahmbatt v CIO* (1984) Imm. A.R. 202).

The 1988 Immigration Act stated what a person who wishes to enter the United Kingdom under a claim of right of abode should produce to the immigration officer (see questions 17 and 223). When entry is dependent on this claim then the person abroad would have a passport or a certificate to this effect and therefore the question of having to decide at the point of entry as to his right of entry based on a right of abode will almost invariably not arise. The question will only arise when the person does not have a British citizen passport or the relevant certificate and wants to take this up with the authorities before coming to the United Kingdom.

The 1988 Act also brought in some restrictions on the exercise of the right of abode by women in cases of polygamy (see questions 17 and 234).

Determining right of abode is complex and anyone who wants to claim this right should seek expert advice and not rely solely on what he understands from this answer.

Q.222 What of the wife of a person with the right of abode?

A.   She has a right of abode under the Immigration Act 1971 if:

    (i) she is a Commonwealth citizen, and

    (ii) she is or has at any time been the wife of a citizen as mentioned in paragraphs (1) and (2), in question 221 above, or

    (iii) she is the wife of a British subject who but for his death would have been a citizen of the United Kingdom and colonies under (1), and (2) of question 221 above when the British Nationality Act 1948 came into force (but not if the husband or herself obtained citizenship by registration after 1948 Act).

By the Immigration Act 1988 S(2) certain restrictions were placed on the right of abode of women and wives in a polygamous marriage. Expert advice must be sought if anyone with right of abode is involved in such a marriage.

Q.223 How does a person prove a right of abode?

A.   The 1988 Immigration Act stated that the person should either produce a United Kingdom passport describing him as a British citizen or as a citizen of the United Kingdom and Colonies having the right of abode in the United Kingdom or should produce a certificate of entitlement issued by, or on behalf of, the United Kingdom government certifying that he has the right of abode. There is no right of appeal whilst in the United Kingdom if the person entering does not have the requisite stamp showing the mentioned passport or certificate and is refused entry.

SPOUSES

Q.224 What is the minimum age for a spouse to be allowed to enter or join the other spouse in the United Kingdom?

A.   Entry clearance will not be granted for any person under 16 years of age to join his/her spouse in the United Kingdom as such for settlement.

Q.225 What are the requirements for one spouse coming with or joining the other spouse who is settled in the United Kingdom?

A.   Where a husband or wife is a British citizen or is already settled (has indefinite leave to remain in the United Kingdom) and either his/her spouse is entering the United Kingdom with him/her or is coming alone to join him/her then the parties must show that:

  (a) the marriage must not have been entered primarily so that the incoming spouse can obtain admission to the United Kingdom;

  (b) the parties must have met;

  (c) each must intend to live with the other as man and wife permanently;

  (d) there must be adequate accommodation for the parties and any dependants without recourse to public funds. Such accommodation must either be owned or occupied exclusively by them. Strictly speaking this means that if they occupy part of a house (such as a flat), it must be adequate and have its own separate amenities like toilet, kitchen, bedrooms, living room, and so forth, and these should not be shared with others not forming part of that family unit. This rule has, however, been made less demanding and it has been accepted by the Home Office that arrangements whereby the applicant joins his/her spouse in a household with other residents are still acceptable providing these requirements are fulfilled and that the applicant and his spouse have at least a small unit of accommodation, such as a bedroom, for their exclusive use. The other requirements are that the accommodation should be owned or legally occupied by the sponsor and it should meet the normal public health provisions, particularly with regard to statutory overcrowding.

  (e) The parties will be able to maintain themselves and any dependants without recourse to public funds. The sponsoring spouse must be able to demonstrate income from a business or employment. Income from a third source, such as from a close family member, might be acceptable as might the offer of immediate employment of the overseas partner by an employer here.

  (f) The incoming spouse must have obtained an entry clearance from his/her country before coming to the United Kingdom and before this can be obtained all the above requirements must be satisfied.

Q.226 What is meant by 'primarily to obtain admission'?

A.   This is a rule where the marriage of an applicant who wishes to enter the United Kingdom with, or to join his spouse for settlement, is tested for genuineness. It is also applicable to those who entered in another capacity, such as a student, visitor, businessman and so forth, and then married here. Where it is found that the marriage between a non-British person and one who is either British or has settled in the United Kingdom was entered into primarily to enable the non-British spouse to gain settlement in the United Kingdom, then such a marriage will not qualify the applicant for entry or to remain. It used to be called a marriage of convenience for the purpose of immigration. The word 'primarily' denotes that the marriage should not be entered into in order to gain entry – it must be a genuine marriage. Where the marriage has been in existence for at least five years before the date of the application or there is a child from the marriage who has a right of abode, the entry clearance officer will not examine the applicant to discover the primary purpose, so long as the marriage is subsisting. Where the marriage has not been in existence for the five years mentioned or there is no child with a right of abode, a great number of questions about this aspect of the marriage may be asked and the same question may be put in a variety of forms in order to find out if the marriage was genuine. Wrong replies by applicants have formed the reasons for a great number of refusals. An example is where a religious tradition or cultural practice calls for the wife to join the husband. In a case involving such persons where the husband is joining his wife in the United Kingdom he may be confronted with this contradiction and the officer may use this as proof of primary purpose and refuse entry. The entry clearance officer may make his own enquiries about the marriage. To be able to prove that the marriage is genuine is not enough; it must be shown that it was also not for the primary purpose of entry. If entry was only an ancillary purpose for the marriage, and not the main or sole purpose, then it should not be deemed, without more evidence, to be a primary purpose marriage. A foreign woman sought a British husband through an agency. After meeting him she fell in love with him and marriage was proposed. The woman insisted on a church wedding after visits by the man to her country some time afterwards. On applying for leave to enter and join her husband she met with a lot of difficulties and was refused leave. On appeal, letters expressing their affection for each other were shown. It was held that primary purpose of the marriage was not in order to be able to enter the United Kingdom; entry was only ancillary and not the main purpose of the marriage (*R v IAT ex parte V.O. Hansford* (1992) Imm.A.R. 407).

Age differences should not be held against a couple as a sole reason for a refusal (*Aida Perez* no. 9636).

In cases of arranged marriages, the reasons given by those involved in the arrangement will be crucial. The arrangers' intention is deemed to be that of the applicant by implication and if their intention to enter was a primary purpose then the marriage will be a primary purpose one (*re Ellahi* no. 9718). In a case where the applicant said it was a love match and it turned out to be an arranged marriage a refusal resulted for not telling the truth. However this does not mean that because it was an arranged marriage it will be automatically deemed to be a primary purpose marriage. Differences in tradition and culture can be explained to the officer. A long period of staying together as husband and wife abroad can help to show devotion to each other and so can having children. If a child was born in the United Kingdom to a spouse settled here, that will help.

A Home Office directive now states that the primary purpose should not be used as a reason for refusal of entry where the marriage has lasted for more than five years or where there are children of the marriage who have the right of abode in the United Kingdom. Finally, it is advisable to seek advice before applying for entry clearance so as to be alert to what the rules are and not to fall foul of them by not quite understanding them (see the postscript).

Q.227 What is meant by 'the parties have met'?

A.   This means they have made one another's 'acquaintance'. It has been held in one case that, where the parties met at a ceremony in which they became betrothed as children aged four and three, that this meeting was not sufficient (*Rewal Raj v ECO New Delhi* 1985) but in another case the couple met at a wedding when aged 12 and 11 and this was sufficient (*re Balvinder Singh* 1986). It would appear that the age of recollection of the other party is a factor to be considered. Marrying a complete stranger without first having met him or her will cause anyone to believe the marriage to be a primary purpose one (see also *Mohd Merharban v ECO (Islamabad)* (1989) Imm.A.R. 57).

Q.228 What else should an applicant be aware of at an interview?

A.   The main reason for an interview is for the entry clearance officer to find out whether the applicant can satisfy all the requirements of the rules relating to his entry for settlement, and it is for the applicant to convince the officer. The less difficult part relates to accommodation and maintenance as these can be proved by documentary evidence. Proving his intention about his marriage and entry into United Kingdom is where the applicant and his sponsor enter into a sticky patch.

Everything that is said in the interview will be written down, so it will be in the applicant's interest to make notes of his answers and be correct and careful.

Whether he is married or coming to get married, he should be able to show letters or videos or pictures (with the dates they were taken) of the partners with each other, and any other evidence that they have been constantly in touch and show affection for each other.

The applicant should discuss the marriage or prospective marriage with the family and the partner so that they do not find themselves saying contradictory things. The best person to have at an interview is the partner and it may prove beneficial if he/she travels to the partner abroad to be together for the interview, if they can afford it. They will both be interviewed separately and it is important to have all the answers agreeing with each other. There is no need to make up answers if one partner cannot remember details; he or she must tell the officer this rather than telling an untruth.

In arranged marriages the parties will be questioned as to what the relationship is between the families. If the families have known each other for a long time and write or visit each other this will be more helpful. Other marriages between the same families can also be helpful as can the fact that both families were in favour of the marriage. The details of the arranged marriage is of importance and should be discussed with the arrangers.

Some marriages are arranged when the children are young. There is no harm in this.

If the other partner is settled in the United Kingdom and the arranged marriage was made after he or she had settled here it will be helpful if it can be shown that the suggestion of an arrangement came from the family of the spouse so settled. If it did not then primary purpose will be more strongly suspected and more proof to the contrary will be required. This, of course, may lead to other questions as to whether the spouse in the United Kingdom was asked whether he or she would live abroad in the applicant's country, why he/she refused, whether it is usual for a man to leave his home and live in his wife's country of settlement or birth or whether it is not usual for this to be the other way round, whether the applicant would have married (or wanted to marry) this person if he had not been living in the United Kingdom, what jobs he would be seeking in the United Kingdom, whether he made enquiries about jobs before the marriage, why he is prepared to give up any job, studies, or other favourable situations in his country to come to the United Kingdom, whether the marriage will break up (or not take place) if entry is refused and the spouse in the United Kingdom refuses to join him abroad, whether he had a choice in entering the marriage, whether the partner is divorced or older or has children of his/her own (in which case why enter such a marriage?), how well or how long he/she has known his/her partner or prospective partner and the family, whether the partner has tried living in his country, and many other questions.

Remember that if the applicant has been married for five years or more, or has a child born in the United Kingdom who is British, then that is most helpful and may involve less rigorous questioning than would otherwise ensue. The other requirements for a spouse to settle must, however, be met. If he has had a refusal before this five year marriage provision or before having a British child, the applicant may make a new application pointing out these facts and at the same time the spouse in the United Kingdom can make representations to this effect.

Q.229   What is considered as 'overcrowding'?

A.   Under statutory laws relating to housing (particularly the Housing Act 1985) overcrowding is an offence that may result in a fine. Accommodation for this purpose consists of 'living accommodation' such as bedrooms and living rooms. It does not include toilets and bathrooms, although a kitchenette with a table and chairs and a folding bed has been considered as 'living accommodation' to be counted in the tests.

There are two tests for overcrowding: the *room standard* and the *space standard*.

The room test, also known as 'sexual overcrowding' test, is applied first. If there is:

one room, two persons are allowed in it; if there are

two rooms, three persons are allowed to share them;

three rooms, five persons are allowed to share them;

four rooms, '7.5 persons' are allowed to share them;

five rooms or more, two persons per room.

Where the number of persons in all the rooms exceed these there is overcrowding.

Where there is no overcrowding under this rule then the inspector will go on to see if the rooms qualify under the other test, the space test. This is done by measuring the space in each room. If the space is:

under 50 sq. ft. no one is allowed (except a child of one year)

between 50 and 70 sq. ft. only 'half a person' is allowed;

between 70 and 90 sq. ft. only one person is allowed;

between 90 and 110 sq. ft. '1.5 persons' are allowed;

over 110 sq. ft. two persons are allowed.

To explain 'half a person' the calculations are made as follows:

adult = 1 unit (or 1 person)

child under 10 = 0.5 unit (half a unit or half a person)

child under 1 = 0 unit.

The number of rooms is then divided by the number of units or persons to give an average. Thus 7.5 persons (or units) will be 7 adults and a child under 10 or 6 adults and 3 children under 10, not counting any child under 1 year. It is quite a complicated procedure but not very difficult to follow. The sponsoring spouse or person will be able to calculate his number of 'living' rooms and how large each is, or he may get the housing inspector to provide a certificate stating his findings so that the sponsor is in a position to say that he will not be in breach of the health requirements relating to housing and over-crowding. Please remember that, in dealing with overcrowding, we are talking of living accommodation exclusively for the family use.

Q.230 What if a marriage took place under customary law?

A.   In some cases – for example, in some customary marriages in west Africa – marriage certificates are not issued. The British Embassy or High Commission may require statutory declarations from both families that a customary marriage has taken place and that the correct procedure was followed as required by custom. The same will apply to a customary law divorce. In other states religious marriage certificates are not issued. Here it may be possible to declare under the marriage legislation that the marriage took place.

Q.231 Will living in Europe before coming to the United Kingdom make a difference?

A.   Whether you have been refused entry as a spouse or for settlement you can use European Union law to gain entry but this is applicable only where the spouse is a British citizen. Such a citizen has the right to go and live and work in an European Union country and has the right to have his spouse join him in that country. The rules about maintenance and accommodation do not apply. A married couple who have lived and worked in a European Union country for some time can then return to the United Kingdom. The British citizen partner must be returning to the United Kingdom to seek work. In this regard it is useful to know that this was the decision in a case brought in the European courts (*Surrinder Singh*) and Immigration officers may sometimes need to be reminded of the European Union implications of this case where they refuse entry (see question 218). In such instances the word spouse is used in the British sense and means a heterosexual spouse. Where, in some countries, marriages are allowed between homosexuals the situation may be slightly different (see question 251 below).

Q232. Will a spouse seeking entry for settlement be given settlement rights upon entry?

A.   No. Such a spouse, if granted entry clearance, will, upon arrival in the United Kingdom, be granted an initial stay not exceeding 12 months. He may work during this period. Before the end of the period granted he may apply for an extension or for settlement. If he applies for an extension only, he may be granted a further 12 months if he continues to satisfy all the requirements mentioned in question 225 above. If he wants settlement then he must apply before the expiry of the initial period given and again, provided he continues to satisfy the requirements, he will be given indefinite leave to remain. A minimum period of 12 months must be completed before settlement can be obtained. The sponsoring spouse, where the other spouse is coming to join him, must be present and 'settled' in the United Kingdom. If he does not obtain settlement lawfully, or is found to have obtained his settlement by deception, then any settlement rights will be forfeited and so may the settlement right of those who gained such rights through him and they will be illegal entrants. (*SSHD v Kalsoom Akhtar, & others* (Th/1732/93 (10755)(determined March 1994)). If the spouse, having been granted the initial 12 months, does not apply for settlement within the period of the said 12 months, he will become an overstayer and will be removed. Recently, obtaining clearance became more cumbersome as a questionnaire is now required to be filled in for applications to remain for the initial year after marriage.

Q.233 What will be the position of a person who entered as a spouse if the marriage breaks down?

A.   A spouse coming with or coming to join another spouse for settlement is given 12 months initially if he and the sponsoring spouse satisfy all the requirements. If, during that period, the marriage breaks down and the parties no longer live together as man and wife then the spouse who was granted leave to remain for one year will have no immigration status to allow him to remain as a spouse and he will have to leave or face deportation. Application can be made by such a spouse to be allowed to remain if he fits into another category or for strong exceptional compassionate grounds, although it is likely that this will be refused. Where the spouses have lived together for 12 months and indefinite leave to remain has been obtained by the spouse applying for it, then his settlement right will no longer be affected even if he becomes divorced or separated. It is only where settlement was obtained by deception – for example, where the parties lied that they were still together to enable the applying spouse to enter – that indefinite leave will be withdrawn. This can, in any case, happen whenever deception has been used and can be proved.

Where the death of the sponsoring spouse occurs before a decision by the Home Office to grant an application for indefinite leave to the foreign spouse, such death will be considered as 'terminating' the marriage and the application will be refused (*SSHD v Mary Connolly* TH/5432/92; see also *Uddin* (11632) and *Harman* (12360)).

POLYGAMOUS SPOUSES

Q.234 What is the position where a man has more than one wife?

A.   A polygamous marriage is not recognised for this purpose. Although such a marriage is recognised as valid where both parties are not domiciled in the United Kingdom and the marriage is acceptable where it was celebrated and according to the domicile of the parties, if one party is domiciled in the United Kingdom such marriage will be void. Domicile is not to be equated with settlement. Someone may be settled in United Kingdom but have a different domicile. For settlement purposes, where a marriage is polygamous (even though valid) another wife will not be allowed in with her husband or to join him if there is already another living wife who is, or has been at any time since her marriage, in the United Kingdom or has been granted right of abode under the Immigration Acts, or was granted an entry clearance to enter as the wife of the husband in such a marriage. It does not matter which wife was the first in line – as long as one wife is here for settlement with her husband, no other wife will be allowed in.

No attempt is made to prevent a polygamous wife who is a British citizen from exercising her right to enter.

For immigration purposes in this context a polygamous marriage is one where the marriage has the potential to be polygamous even though at its inception neither party had any other spouse. It is this liberty for polygamy that is essential (although the reasoning for this is difficult to see in view of the fact that since 1988 only one wife can be allowed in to settle). If, however, one wife is here as a visitor when the other wife enters with or joins her husband, the presence of the visiting wife will be disregarded.

Q.235   Can another wife enter as a visitor?

A.   There is no reason why the other wife of a polygamous marriage cannot enter as a visitor if she satisfies all the requirements for this category, particularly that of having an intention of returning to her country overseas at the end of the period granted her. If she has children overseas, or any other strong and plausible reason that will make it imperative for her to return, this should be shown.

Q.236   What is the position of children of polygamous marriages?

A.   The right of abode of children of polygamous marriages is not affected. A child of a marriage valid in England, whether polygamous or not, may be a British citizen by descent. In some instances, even where the marriage is not deemed to be valid in the United Kingdom, the child may be deemed to be legitimate and therefore British. Where a child is not British then entry will depend on whether both parents are present and settled in the United Kingdom otherwise, if only one parent is settled, then the 'sole responsibility' rule will apply.

FIANCÉ(E)S

Q.237.   What is the position of those coming to get married?

A.   The requirements are more or less the same for someone coming to get married here as for those already married and coming with, or coming to join, their partners already settled here. The parties should show that neither is married and that they are eligible to get married. A divorcee should show evidence of a legal divorce. A widow or widower should provide evidence of the death of her former spouse or, where there was an annulment, a certificate proving this should be made available. Originals of any such certificates will be required but where such originals have been lost a statutory declaration may be acceptable, although this method will be less favourably accepted.

All the points mentioned in the answers dealing with entry for a spouse should be heeded when going for an interview for an entry clearance (see 'Postscript').

Q.238 How long will a fiancé(e) be given to remain in the United Kingdom?

A. Such a person will be admitted for a period not exceeding six months to enable the marriage to take place. There will be a prohibition from employment.

Q.239 What happens if the marriage does not take place within the period granted?

A. In such a case the fiancé(e) given the six months leave to remain may apply for an extension but such application must be made before the expiry of the said period. He must then show good cause why the marriage did not take place during the six months and will have to produce evidence that the marriage will take place at an early date whilst still continuing to satisfy all the other requirements as mentioned previously. If the Home Office is satisfied with the reasons and the arrangements made it may grant a further period of stay that is appropriate, considering all the reasons put forward, to enable the parties to get married.

CHILDREN

Q.240 What are the requirements for a child whose parent or parents or relative is settled in the United Kingdom?

A. Such a child must be under 18 years and must not be leading an independent life, must not be married, and must not have formed an independent family unit. Both his parents must be lawfully present and settled in the United Kingdom if he is coming to join them (if the sponsoring parent(s) are not lawfully in possession of settlement rights they will be illegal entrants). Where he is accompanying them they must be coming for settlement.

Where only one parent is present and settled in the United Kingdom and the other parent is not, and the child alone is seeking admission to join or accompany the parent in the United Kingdom, admission for settlement will be refused unless the parent in the United Kingdom has had 'sole responsibility' for the child's upbringing or the other parent outside the United Kingdom is dead.

Where the parent outside the United Kingdom is alive then admission may be granted to the child to enter and settle with the parent in the United Kingdom only if there are serious and compelling reasons which will make exclusion of the child undesirable. Where, however, the child is under 12 years it may be possible to obtain admission without the 'sole responsibility' test being applied. In such a case one parent or, in the absence of a parent, a relative may be able to have the child but such parent or relative in the United Kingdom must have made suitable arrangements for the child's care. If the one parent is the father then a female relative must be resident in the household and she should be capable of looking after the child and willing to do so. Such a woman need not be married to the child's father and can be a so-called 'common-law wife'. This is only a concession and can be refused.

All the other usual requirements for adequate and exclusive accommodation and maintenance without recourse to public funds will have to be satisfied.

An entry clearance must first be applied for and obtained abroad before coming to the United Kingdom for settlement, and indefinite leave to remain will be granted on arrival.

**Q.241	If a child was born in the United Kingdom will he have to qualify in the same way as mentioned above?**

A.	Where a child was born in the United Kingdom on or after 1 January 1983 but is not a British citizen then there is a slight advantage in that there is no need for both parents to have been given leave to enter or remain. If one or both parents are seeking leave to enter, or have entered and been given leave to remain for a limited period, the child may enter with or join the parents or parent and his leave will be for the same period as that of the parent with the longer period. Where the parents are living apart then the period will be the same as that of the parent with the day-to-day care of the child.

Where one parent has the right of abode, or is a British citizen, then the child may enter with or join his parent (or parents) in the United Kingdom. The 'sole responsibility' rule will not apply if there is only one parent in the United Kingdom provided that parent is a British citizen or has a right of abode.

The other requirements are the same: the child must be under 18 years, unmarried, not living an independent life, and should not have formed a family unit of his own. Because such a child, with a British parent or a parent with a right of abode in the United Kingdom (see questions 221–223 above), would have had the right of residence in the United Kingdom then, if he leaves the United Kingdom and application is then made for him to re-enter, he would be treated in the same way as a returning resident and would be allowed in if he had not been away from the United Kingdom for longer than two years (see questions 253 *et seq* on returning residents, below).

Indefinite leave to remain will be granted if the parent is a British citizen or has the right of abode.

Q.242 What is meant by 'sole responsibility'?

A.   This is where one parent has responsibility for the child and such responsibility is not shared. There must also be genuine affection and interest in the child and cogent evidence of this must be shown (see *in re Rudolph* (1984) Imm.A.R. 84 and also *R v IAT. ex parte Sajid Mahmood* (1988) Imm.A.R. 121 regarding 'sole responsibility'). If that parent shares the responsibility with another person (for example, where the other parent always maintained the child) then it is not sole responsibility (*Eugene v ECO (Bridgetown, Barbados)*(1975) Imm.A.R. 111). On the other hand, the assumption of financial responsibility by itself is not conclusive evidence of sole responsibility (*Ravat & others v ECO (Bombay)* (1974) Imm.A.R. 79). Shared responsibility will be assumed if the child does not live with the one parent but lives instead with the grandparents, even if there is close and regular contact with the child by the parent. 'There are matters of day-to-day decisions in the upbringing of the child . . . to be decided on the spot by whoever is looking after the child' (*Ramos* 1989 I.A.R. 148). In one case, even though the mother was providing financial support for the child and grandparents, entry was refused.

Where both parents are in the United Kingdom but only one parent is settled, then the child will not be granted settlement, and entry for settlement will be refused where one parent is bringing the child in and is returning and not settling here.

Q.243 Will a child of a woman in a polygamous marriage be allowed to enter for settlement?

A.   Where a child's mother is a party to a polygamous marriage such a child will be refused entry for settlement just as his mother would be if there were another woman living who is the wife of the husband and who has at any time since the marriage been in the United Kingdom.

ADOPTED CHILDREN

Please note that adoption is a very complicated matter and it becomes more complicated within the ambit of immigration. Anyone seeking to adopt a child abroad to bring to the United Kingdom, or even someone adopting a foreign child in the United Kingdom, should seek special advice. These answers only provide a brief overview of the rules and requirements.

Q.244 Can an adopted child come to settle in the United Kingdom?

A.   Yes. The requirements for natural children apply as well as certain other requirements. Where both parents are coming to the United Kingdom for settlement, or where they have both already entered and settled, or where one parent is already settled and the other is coming to join the parent already settled here, the adopted child may be allowed to come in with them or join them.

The 'sole responsibility' rule will apply when bringing the adopted child into the United Kingdom – the child will be allowed in where only one adoptive parent is settled in the United Kingdom and has the sole responsibility for the child. Alternatively, if only one parent is alive and settled and the other is dead, the adopted child will be allowed in.

The other common rules that the child must be under 18, unmarried, should not have formed an independent family unit of his own, and should not be living independently of his adoptive parents, also apply. The usual requirements for adequate maintenance and exclusive accommodation without recourse to public funds will have to be satisfied. In addition to all these points, the adoption must have complied with certain conditions:

(i) The adoption must have been in accordance with the laws of the country of the adopted child's origin or residence.

(ii) The adoption must take place when both adoptive parents are resident abroad. If one or both adoptive parents were settled in the United Kingdom and the child was adopted due to the inability of the natural parents to care for him (or where the child has been in the care of someone other than the natural parents) there must be a genuine transfer of parental (or the carer's) responsibility and all ties with the natural family (or carer) must be lost or broken.

(iii) An adopted child of adoptive parent or parents settled in the United Kingdom must have the same rights and obligations as any other child of the marriage. Just as a spouse wishing to enter with, or join, the other spouse here should not have entered into a marriage mainly to obtain entry, so adoption must not have been mainly or solely in order to enable a child to gain entry to the United Kingdom. Such a child must not be adopted in order to facilitate his entry into, or his stay in, the United Kingdom, or with a view to obtaining British nationality or a right of abode. It must be to serve the welfare and security of the child (*re K (Adoption: non-patrial)* (1994) 2 FCR 617).

All the above requirements must be fully satisfied when applying for an entry clearance, which must be obtained by the child before entering the United Kingdom if he was adopted abroad.

Q.245 Are adoptions in any country of origin of the child considered valid in the United Kingdom?

A.   Adoption can be specified as an overseas adoption by order of the Secretary of State. The Secretary of State can certify that an adoption abroad is lawful. Under the Adoption (Designation of Overseas Adoption) Order 1973, adoptions made by orders of courts of law in some countries are considered valid in Britain. These are:

Anguilla, Australia, Bahamas, Barbados, Belize, Bermuda, Botswana, British Virgin Islands, Canada, Cayman Islands, Cyprus, Dominica, Fiji, Ghana, Gibraltar, Guyana, Hong Kong, Jamaica, Kenya, Lesotho, Malawi, Malaysia, Malta, Mauritius, Montserrat, New Zealand, Nigeria, Pitcairn Islands, St Christopher and Nevis, St Vincent, Seychelles, Singapore, Sri Lanka, Swaziland, Tanzania, Tonga, Trinidad and Tobago, Uganda, Zambia, Zimbabwe.

All the above countries are Commonwealth countries but not all Commonwealth countries have adoption enactments (Sierra Leone does not, for example) and adoptions are *de facto*. The other countries in the order are:

Austria, Belgium, Denmark (including Greenland and the Faroes), Finland, France (including Reunion, Martinique, Guadeloupe and French Guyana), Germany, Greece, Iceland, Republic of Ireland, Israel, Italy, Luxembourg, Namibia, the Netherlands (and Antilles), Norway, Portugal (and the Azores and Madeira), South Africa (now a Commonwealth country), Spain (including the Canary Islands and the Balearic Islands), Surinam, Sweden, Swaziland, Turkey, the United States of America, and some countries of the former Yugoslavia.

Q.246 What is the position where there are no adoption laws in the country of origin of the child?

A.   There is no strict rule that such a child has to be 'legally adopted'.

Under the Immigration Act 1971 'legally adopted' means adopted in pursuance of an order made by any court of law in the United Kingdom and islands or by any adoption specified as an overseas adoption by order of the Secretary of State under section 4 of the Adoption Act 1968. The Secretary of State can certify that an adoption abroad is lawful as mentioned above. In cases which do not fall within those countries named then it is more difficult to show adoption. Notification of intention to adopt must be given to the Social Services Department together with legal proof that the child is available for adoption, that the adoption is not against the wishes of the natural parents, and that no payment has been made or accepted as a reward for the adoption. In some countries where there is no enactment or procedure for adoption a party may be able to apply to a court of law to make an order, after taking evidence from all the parties, to allow the child to be a ward of the applicant. The court may grant permission to take the child out of its jurisdiction. This is not the same as an adoption but, with evidence that the natural parents intended this to be an adoption and that all ties have been broken with the natural parents, that the adoptive parents are now the parents of the child, that there are no reasons why the child should not be admitted to the United Kingdom under the immigration rules, that it is in the best interest of the child to be adopted, and there are no reasons why a United Kingdom court will not grant an adoption order, then it may be possible to have a court in the United Kingdom grant an adoption order. There is a very long questionnaire to be filled in for the Home Office when applying for a child from abroad to enter the United Kingdom for adoption. Medical information about the child, the natural parents, and the adoptive parents is essential.

Q.247 What becomes of the nationality of the adopted child?

A.   A child who is not a British citizen and who is adopted by a court order made in the United Kingdom becomes a British citizen as soon as the order is made if one of the adoptive parents is British (British Nationality Act 1981 s1(5)). He is then in the same position as a citizen by birth. A child who is a British citizen by descent and is adopted cannot change his citizenship. He remains a British citizen by descent.

OTHER RELATIVES

Q.248 What other relatives may be allowed to settle in the United Kingdom?

A.   The rules allow for the admission of widowed mothers and widowed fathers aged 65 or over. They also allow for parents travelling together or grandparents travelling together if at least one of is 65 or over. In certain cases parents and grandparents under 65 may be allowed in. In some cases the rules may allow sons and daughters, sisters, brothers, uncles and aunts over 18.

Q.249 What are the requirements for relatives to enter?

A. The requirements are that such a relative should be related to someone present and settled in the United Kingdom.
The relationship is one of the following:

(i) mother or grandmother who is a widow and aged 65 or over; or

(ii) father or grandfather who is a widower aged 65 or over; or

(iii) parents or grandparents travelling together of whom one is 65 or over; or

(iv) a parent or grandparent who is 65 or over and who has remarried but who cannot depend on a spouse or the child(ren) of the second marriage for financial support. The person settled in the United Kingdom must be able and willing to maintain the parent or grandparent and any spouse and child(ren) of this second marriage who would be admissible as a dependant; or

(v) a parent or grandparent under 65 and living alone abroad, in the most exceptional compassionate circumstances and mainly financially dependent on relatives settled in the United Kingdom. Where the above mentioned relationship exists then such person must either be joining the person settled in the United Kingdom or accompanying the relative in order to settle. The dependent relative must be wholly or mainly financially dependent on the sponsoring relative in the United Kingdom. Financial dependence must not have been deliberately created (*Zam v ECO, Lahore* (1973)). The sponsoring relative must be able and willing to adequately maintain and accommodate the relative without recourse to public funds in accommodation owned or occupied exclusively by him.

The incoming relative must not have any close relative in his own country to whom he could turn to for financial help (see *R v IAT ex parte Sayana Khatum* (1989) Imm.A.R. 482). This has been held to mean a relative who had the ability to provide some assistance by way of a house or financial help to make it reasonable to expect the applicant to depend upon that relative rather than a relative in the United Kingdom (*R v IAT ex parte Bastiampillai* (1983)). Such relative must not only have the ability but must also be willing to provide support (*R v IAT ex parte Dadhibhai* (1983)). Compliance with all these conditions must be proved to the satisfaction of the ECO abroad and an entry clearance must be obtained for this purpose before arriving in the United Kingdom. Indefinite leave to remain (settlement) may then be granted upon entry.

Q.250 What of the other members of the family: sons and daughters over 18, brothers, sisters, aunts, uncles, and so forth?

A.   The sponsoring relative must show exceptional compassionate circumstances for the Home Office to allow such a relative in to settle. In addition there must be evidence of the required financial resources, maintenance and accommodation as mentioned above. Sons and daughters over 18 must also not have formed a family unit of their own or be living independently and must have no close relative to turn to for help, as is also the case with the other relatives mentioned. Such over-age children may be allowed in with their parents only if refusing them entry would cause hardship. Where there is only one over-age 'child' amongst many other children he/she may be allowed in if refusing entry would cause hardship. The older the over-age 'child' is, however, the more difficult it will be for the Home Office to exercise its discretion. All the other requirements (such as accommodation and maintenance) must also be satisfied.

HOMOSEXUALS

Q.251 What is the position relating to homosexuals?

A.   The situation relating to 'gay' men is the same as for lesbians. There is no provision in the rules for gays or lesbians to bring in their partners for settlement in the same way as married heterosexuals can bring in their spouses. The new rules mention 'spouse' in the terms of being a person who is legally married within the laws of the UK. The word 'spouse' is used in the British sense and means a heterosexual one.

In a few countries, such as Holland and Denmark, marriages are allowed between homosexuals and the situation may be slightly different under expanded European Union law. However, under the rules, such a 'spouse' (although lawfully married abroad as may also be the case of a heterosexual marriage where a spouse is under 16) will not be allowed in to settle as a 'spouse'. In one exceptional case the 'partner' was allowed in 'outside the rules' because of 'exceptional compassionate circumstances' after the Immigration Appeals Tribunal and the Court of Appeal had turned down the appeal (*R v IAT ex parte Wirdestedt* (1990) Imm.A.R. 20).

Recently two women were married officially. However there was a legal loophole as one of the 'women' had had a sex-change from male to female but was officially still registered as 'male'. Thus, technically, this was a marriage between a male and a female.

COHABITATION

Q.252 If a male and female person are living together but are not married, what is their position?

A. The Home Office has a discretion to allow people who are not married to enter. This will be a concession 'outside the rules'. Cohabitation is not looked upon in the same way as a homosexual relationship. This is because English common law recognises heterosexual relationships. Only monogamous cohabitation is recognised.

Where there is conclusive evidence that a genuine and subsisting common-law relationship akin to marriage exists, it should be considered under the same rules as apply to marriage. This may make an application less onerous for such a common-law spouse, particularly where there are children from such a relationship (although the absence of a child does not mean that the couple do not cohabit or that they are not devoted to each other). The fact that the couple have been living together (for at least two years) and continue to do so is a strong reason for not refusing entry. Where both parties are free to marry but they choose not to, this should not lessen their chances of entry. Even where one party is temporarily tied, this should not reduce the couple's chances of entry if the relationship is stable.

All the other requirements applicable to a spouse must also be satisfied. Children of such a relationship, aged under 18, will be required to satisfy the same conditions for entry and settlement as children of a married couple.

The person applying to enter will have his/her entry clearance stamped with 'accompanying/joining Mr/Mrs/Miss'. The Home Office may consider applications from within Britain without requiring the common-law spouse to return overseas to apply for entry clearance. The common-law spouse will be allowed the same period as a married spouse – 12 months initially – and application may be made, before the expiry of this period, for indefinite leave to remain (see postscript).

RETURNING RESIDENTS

Q.253 Who are considered as returning residents?

A.   A returning resident is one who had indefinite leave to remain in the United Kingdom and then left and is returning to the United Kingdom. This person must have had indefinite leave to remain when he last left the United Kingdom. His absence from the United Kingdom must not be longer than two years and he must now be seeking leave to re-enter the United Kingdom. Such re-entry must be with the intention of settling in the United Kingdom. (In short, this intention is the same as when he obtained indefinite leave to remain before his period of absence and is affirming his intention to continue to be settled.) If he states or shows an intention not to settle he will be refused entry as a returning resident. When he last left the United Kingdom he must not have depended on public funds to be able to leave. (See *ex parte Coomasuru* (1983) Imm.A.R. and also *ex parte Tolba* (1988) Imm.A.R. 78.)

Q.254 Does a returning resident need an entry clearance or visa?

A.   So long as the requirements mentioned above have been met such a person does not need either from abroad. He will need to satisfy the immigration officer at the entry point that he had indefinite leave to remain before he left, that he has been away for less than two years, that he left the United Kingdom unaided by public funds, and that he is returning for settlement. If he is using a new passport that does not confirm his residential status it will be advisable for him to have the old passport with him as well in order to show the authorities that he had indefinite leave to remain before he left. Alternatively, he must have some evidence of his previous residential status (for example, the letter from the Home Office that usually accompanies granting of this status).

Q.255 What is the position of a returning resident who has stayed abroad for longer than two years?

A.   Such a person may be allowed back in as a returning resident with indefinite leave to remain if he has stayed away for longer than two years. In such a case, long residence in the United Kingdom before he left (for example, if he has spent most of his life in the United Kingdom), or strong and close connections with the United Kingdom, will be helpful (see *ex parte Muhammad Safiulah* (1986) Imm.A.R.

424; *ex parte Ademuyiwa* (1986) Imm.A.R. 1; *ex parte Agyen-Frempong* (1986) Imm.A.R. 108).

The longer he has been away, the stronger and closer must be the ties with the United Kingdom. The continuation of whatever reason led to him being granted indefinite leave to remain in the first place can be important (for example, if he was originally given leave to remain because he is married to a British citizen or someone settled in the United Kingdom and this is still the case, although he will have to show strong reasons for leaving his spouse for so long and will have to demonstrate that he maintained close ties whilst away). Having a home in the United Kingdom, and an intention to remain and live in this home, will be considered.

Force majeure cannot always be relied on as a reason for staying away beyond the allowed period. Death in the family or loss of travelling documents may be considered if the excess period was a reasonable one under the circumstances and has not resulted in long over-staying abroad. Visa nationals (and even non-visa nationals) are advised to obtain entry clearance before coming back if they have exceeded the two year period.

Q.256 Do the same rules apply to British citizens who have been away for over two years?

A.   No. A British citizen passport holder is not subject to immigration rules and can go and come as he likes. The same applies to a British overseas citizen who has been admitted for settlement. He has the right of readmission at any time and the returning resident rule does not apply. Such a citizen can ask the Home Office to have an endorsement on his passport to that effect, and it is advisable to have this endorsement.

Q.257 What if a person who claims entry as a returning resident is given leave to enter for a limited period?

A.   In this case, say for example that he was admitted the second time as a student or visitor or businessman, he would have lost his status as having indefinite leave to remain and his rights to a claim on the grounds of being a returning resident would be lost. He can only stay in the category under which he was admitted and will have to leave at the end of the period granted under that category. To regain the status of settlement he will have to apply to enter all over again and stay long enough to be able to obtain indefinite leave to remain.

This can prove more difficult than it seems unless he is applying as the spouse of a citizen coming to or residing in the United Kingdom (in which case he should have been able to satisfy the immigration authorities to let him in as a returning resident and not as a student or visitor or businessman or any other category that carries limited stay). The rules provide for a person aggrieved by imposition of a time limit or condition on entry to apply to the Home Office for variation, and to appeal against a refusal to vary, provided certain conditions are met.

HOLDERS OF SPECIAL VOUCHERS

Q.258 Who may become holders of special vouchers ?

They are British overseas citizens and are either issued with a special voucher by a British government representative abroad or have been issued with an entry clearance for settlement in the United Kingdom as a voucher holder. This voucher will not be available to those with dual nationality or those who are eligible for dual nationality. Holders of vouchers must be heads of households and there must be pressure on such persons to leave their country. This type of voucher, granting permission to settle in the United Kingdom, was set up to help those with east African connections who are under pressure to leave their own countries. This category includes British protected persons and British subjects but it does not include British dependent territories citizens.

Q.259 What are the benefits of having a special voucher?

A.   Holders of vouchers obtain rights of settlement immediately upon arrival in the United Kingdom, provided they are British overseas citizens and that the vouchers, or an entry clearance for settlement, have been issued by a British government representative overseas (a High Commission or Embassy representative or other authorised representative).

Q.260 Can a special voucher holder bring his spouse and children to join him?

A.   Yes. If they had not been granted such clearance when the voucher holder obtained permission, he can apply to bring them in if he can show that he can adequately accommodate and maintain them without recourse to public funds. They will also obtain indefinite leave to remain. Entry clearances must be obtained for them before they come to the United Kingdom.

CONCESSIONS

Q.261 Are there any concessions granted for someone to settle after long period of residence in the United Kingdom?

A.   Under the rules there are no provisions for someone to be granted indefinite leave to remain due to a long stay in the United Kingdom. The Home Office has discretion in a case where a person has been continuously resident in United Kingdom, lawfully, for 10 years or more and each case will depend on its merits. Short absences abroad, up to six months, will not breach the 'continuous stay' requirement unless the individual did not intend to return or had not established ties with the United Kingdom. A series of short breaks abroad in the period of a year, which show the person to be spending more time abroad than in the United Kingdom, may be regarded as breaking continuity of residence. Reasonable periods of absence for a holiday or business may be allowed. Close ties with the United Kingdom after lengthy residence will be taken into account. Expelling someone who has resided here for such a period will mainly occur where he poses a serious threat to public safety, public health, or public morality.

Where the person can show continuous residence for at least 14 years then the Home Office may grant him indefinite leave to remain even if such a stay was not in compliance with immigration rules or requirements provided there no criminal record and no deliberate attempt to evade or circumvent immigration control. This concession requires the actual physical presence of the person in the United Kingdom to satisfy the residency aspect (see *ex parte Samuel Ogunbodede* (1993) Imm.A.R. 28). Any time spent in the United Kingdom free from immigration control (for example, in diplomatic service) may count towards the period of residence but only after the person concerned has ceased to be exempt. Length of residence is only one of the factors that will be considered and any close ties will be viewed in relation to the individual's ties elsewhere. The concessions for unmarried daughters over 18 and under 21 still forming part of the family has now been removed and they can only be considered under 'compassionate' grounds (see question 250). Each case will be determined on its own facts (*ex parte Musah* (1994) Imm.A.R. 395, *re Frederick* (11747)). For concessions relating to children under 12 coming to a private fee-paying school see above and see question 240.

Q.262 In all the cases of settlement mentioned above what effect will settlement have on the citizenship of the persons who have settled?

A.   The answer is none. Anyone who comes into the United Kingdom to settle will keep his original citizenship and does not become a British citizen merely by settling in the United Kingdom. He can stay as long as he wishes but this will not entitle him to British citizenship unless he applies for it and satisfies all the conditions required. See under Chapter 12, 'British nationality'.

Chapter 9

Asylum

Q.263 Who is an asylum seeker?

A. He is someone applying for asylum in the United Kingdom who claims to be a refugee as defined by the United Nations Convention and Protocol relating to the Status of Refugees which has been signed by the United Kingdom. This creates obligations preventing the United Kingdom from making such an applicant leave Britain. Under the rules this includes persons with a well-founded fear of persecution for reasons of race, religion, nationality, membership of a particular social group, or political opinion. Such a person must be outside the country of his nationality and have a genuine fear for his life or freedom on returning or, not having a nationality and being outside the country of his habitual residence, must be unwilling to return for the same reasons. An application for asylum is an application for leave to enter (*R v IAT ex parte SSHD* [1990] 1 WLR 1126).

Q.264 Who determines the application?

A. As soon as an application is made, the matter is passed on to the Home Secretary who takes the decision. The immigration officer does not decide these applications and cannot refuse the applicant outright without referring the matter for a decision by the Home Office. If the result is a refusal there is a right of appeal to a special adjudicator and then up the judicial appeals ladder. Time limits for appeals can be very short, particularly against claims certified to be 'without foundation' ('fast track' appeals have to be made within two days).

Q.265 What rules govern the granting of asylum?

A. When the application reaches the Secretary of State, he will have to satisfy himself that the asylum seeker has arrived at a port of entry in the United Kingdom or is in the United Kingdom. He will then look to see if he is a refugee as defined by the Convention mentioned earlier and will decide whether a refusal will result in his being required to go to a country in which his life or freedom would be threatened on account of his race, religion, nationality, political opinion, or membership of a particular social group. If a refusal will result in such a threat it will be in breach of the Convention.

Where the asylum seeker came through a 'third country' the Secretary of State will have to satisfy himself that removal to that third country will not raise any questions under the Convention. In this sense it is understood that the first country is the country of the applicant, the second country is the United Kingdom and the 'third country' is one in which the applicant passed through before arriving in the United Kingdom.

According to the rules, failure of an asylum seeker, without reasonable explanation, to make a prompt and full disclosure of all the facts material to his case, either in writing, orally, or otherwise, so as to assist the Home Office fully to establish the facts, may lead to a refusal. This involves complying with any requirement to fill in a questionnaire, or to report to a particular place for an interview or to be fingerprinted.

Any act which will damage the asylum seeker's credibility will be taken into account if no reasonable explanation is forthcoming and such acts include the following:

(a) failure to apply immediately upon arrival (unless the reason is that the events which made him apply for asylum after entering the United Kingdom occurred after his arrival and since his entry);

(b) false representation;

(c) the destruction, damage or disposal of any passport or other document or ticket relevant to his claim;

(d) activities undertaken by the applicant in the United Kingdom either before or after lodging his application for asylum which are not consistent with his previous beliefs and behaviour and are calculated to create or substantially enhance his claim;

(e) any concurrent or other asylum application made in any other country.

Any act of anyone acting as an agent for the applicant relating to the points mentioned above may also be taken into consideration.

The rules also state that a refusal may result if there is any part of the country from which the applicant claims to be a refugee in which he would not have a well-founded fear of persecution and to which he could reasonably be expected to go (see question 277 below).

Where a group of people is seeking asylum, and such group does not fall within the criteria laid down by the Convention and Protocol, all the individuals in the group will be refused unless there is some evidence pertaining to any one individual which distinguishes and differentiates his claim from that of the group. Any of the above may result in the Home Office certifying that the claim 'is without foundation' (this applies particularly to those coming through third countries).

If an applicant does qualify under the UNHCR criteria but there are non-Convention and Protocol reasons for fear of returning, the Home Office may consider exceptional leave to remain.

Q.266 What happens to the applicant when he makes the application?

A.   He is either detained or is given temporary admission where there is reasonable cause to believe that the applicant will not disappear, but such admission will be subject to certain requirements such as possessing a known address with relatives or friends who may vouch for the applicant at any time required. He will be fingerprinted. Detention is often in a detention centre but in many cases applicants are detained in ordinary prisons and often treatment is not much different from prisoners' treatment. The applicant will be interviewed or, where he is given temporary admission, will be given a form to fill in and return by a fixed date.

If necessary he will be interviewed again. During the period while his application is being considered – which may take up to two years or even longer – the immigration authorities may issue a standard form or letter acknowledging that he has applied for asylum and that it is under consideration, and that he is not to take up employment (paid or unpaid) until six months after his application, and then only after obtaining permission to do so.

The form will contain the applicant's photograph, address, passport number (if he had one), nationality, date and place of arrival, and a home office reference number and stamp. If his application is successful he is then given refugee status with all the benefits that this entails. If he is refused he will be notified of the refusal and the reason for the refusal and will be given another interview before his removal from the United Kingdom. The applicant will have a right of appeal to a special adjudicator.

In some cases the Home Office uses its discretion and grants exceptional leave to remain. This is outside the rules and there is no appeal against any refusal of this temporary measure (see question 267).

Those granted exceptional leave to remain are expected to use their own passports unless they are refused such passports or renewals by their countries in which case they can obtain a travel document from the United Kingdom.

Q.267 What is exceptional leave to remain?

A.   Exceptional leave to remain is granted at the discretion of the Home Office and cannot be applied for under the immigration rules as a matter of right. It is only granted in asylum cases where those seeking asylum are refused but the Home Office does not consider it safe for them to be sent back at this time. The Secretary of State for Home Affairs may then grant such persons 'exceptional leave to remain' until he decides otherwise or until it is considered safe for the applicants to go back. The leave will initially be for one year and then the application will be reconsidered. If the danger still exists a further period of three years will be granted and, again after consideration, a further three years may be given and thereafter indefinite leave to remain may be granted (after seven years' residence – the various periods mentioned can be varied). In certain cases settlement may be granted before the seven years.

Q.268 What is the policy towards granting settlement to one with exceptional leave to remain wishing to bring his family to join him?

A.   As exceptional leave to remain is only a temporary measure to allow asylum seekers to remain usually until the situation they were escaping from no longer applies, after which they are returned to their countries, the issue of settlement in the United Kingdom for such people and their families does not arise. As mentioned in the previous answer, certain cases may be considered for settlement before the seven-year period and, where an application is made for a spouse or minor children to join the person with exceptional leave to remain, this is usually considered after only four years, subject to the general rules applicable for admission of spouses and dependants already mentioned above. The application, of course, can be considered if made earlier than four years if it is based on exceptional compassionate circumstances. (see *R v SSHD ex parte Muslu* (1993) Imm.A.R. 151). The situation in certain countries can become notorious and applicants from such countries may be granted exceptional leave to remain fairly easily.

Q.269 What is 'well founded fear of persecution'?

A.   This means a serious possibility or a reasonable degree of likelihood (on the balance of probabilities) of an individual being persecuted if he returns to his country (*re Sivakumaran* (1988) Imm.A.R. 147). The asylum seeker's 'well-founded fear' must be in relation to his own country.

Persecution can take the form of a threat to life or freedom or other serious violation of human rights, or a situation causing the asylum seeker to fear for his safety, and these conditions can arise in a variety of ways. It is not possible to categorise them. Each case depends on its own merits.

Persecution does not mean prosecution, so if an applicant ran away from his country because of fear of prosecution for a criminal offence he cannot claim asylum unless such prosecution is due to his political or other opinion which falls within the ambit defined by the Convention and Protocol as shown in question 263 above. The test is whether an illegal or criminal act amounts simply to a criminal act rather than to a political campaign which could found a claim for asylum.

The reasons for such fear to be well founded must be provided by the applicant. The asylum seeker must not only be in fear but must show that the reason for such fear exists. The fear need not be based on the applicant's own experiences and if he can show that his fear is based on what has happened to others in a similar position to him (for example, relatives, friends or others belonging to his social or political or racial or ethnic group) then his fear that the same persecution will befall him may be 'well founded'.

Avoiding probable persecution may be considered. Serious violation of human rights may also provide grounds for such fears. Discrimination may also amount to persecution if 'the measures of discrimination lead to consequences of a substantially prejudicial nature for persons concerned, e.g. serious restrictions on his rights to earn a livelihood ...' (*UNHCR Handbook; SSHD v Adrian G. Chiver*, Appeal no, HX/70386/93 (case no. 10758) determined on 24 March 1994).

Even where the discrimination is not perpetrated by the authorities but the authorities are not able to offer effective protection from serious discrimination or other offensive acts, or where they tolerate such discrimination, this should be regarded as persecution (*Re. Grahovac* (11761), see also *re. Kaja* (11038) and *re. Asuming* (11530), and *re. Savchenkov* (11513)).

Q.270 What is meant by 'a particular social group'?

A.   There is no particular definition and this aspect is quite difficult to show. Generally speaking the UNHCR has stated that persons of similar background, habits, or social status can be within a particular social group. Some cases involving homosexuals have been accepted as falling within this category where in their particular country of origin such a group is banned and their social habit is unlawful.

In another situation it has been accepted that Westernised women in some countries are considered to be in danger of persecution. In such cases applicants are more likely to be given exceptional leave to remain until the situation changes. For cases involving social groups see the above-mentioned cases as well as *re Macgregor* (1789), *re Ahari* (7333).

Q.271 What if there has been a previous application in another country?

A. The rules state that where a previous application in another country which is a party to the United Nations Convention and Protocol relating to the Status of Refugees was considered and rejected, then that person's subsequent application in the United Kingdom will be refused and he will be returned to that country and invited to raise any new circumstances with the authorities in that country.

Where he had made a previous application in the United Kingdom and had been refused, any subsequent application will have to show a substantial change of circumstances since the date of his previous application.

Q.272 Can the wife and children and dependants of an applicant be included in the application for asylum?

A. A spouse, or minor children (under 18), or dependants may be included in the application by the principal applicant. Where the principal's application succeeds, the others will be given the same approval. In such a case it will be necessary to establish the identity of the children but they will not be interviewed.

Q.273 Can children apply for asylum if they are not accompanied by parents?

A. Yes. Because of their tender age and vulnerability particular attention is given to their cases which are handled as a matter of priority. More weight is given to indications of risk than to the child's state of mind and his understanding of his situation. Thus the welfare of a young child will be of considerable importance and an application will not be refused merely because the child does not understand his situation or because the child has not formed a well-founded fear of persecution.

If evidence of the substance of his claim can be obtained without interviewing the child then this line will be pursued (by written enquiries or from other sources, for example). If such evidence is not available and an interview has to be carried out, it will be conducted in the presence of a representative or an adult who for the time being takes responsibility. Such an adult should not be a police or immigration officer. An interview should not be carried out when the child is distressed, or tired, or confused, or alarmed. When it is carried out it should be conducted at the child's own pace and the child should be allowed to express himself in his own way.

Q.274 Can a person apply from overseas for asylum in the United Kingdom?

A. Where the asylum seeker is applying from his own country it does not fall within the ambit of the UN Convention and Protocol relating to the Status of Refugees and there are no rules for application for this status in the immigration rules. Any consideration of such a case will be exceptional and 'outside the rules'.

Where an applicant has escaped to another country, he should make his application in that country unless he can show that the country is also not a safe place for him. This is known as a 'third country' application and unless he can show strong links with the United Kingdom (see question 275) it will be refused.

In circumstances where a person has already been granted refugee status in the United Kingdom, his spouse and family (children under 18) living abroad may apply, free of charge, for entry clearance to join him. If only exceptional leave to remain was granted then the spouse and children will not normally be granted entry until the person here has had four years of exceptional leave.

One final rare situation is where the government has recognised certain people in named countries as 'refugees' and a quota is given to allow entry clearance to be given to such people to enter as refugees, initially for four years, after which they can apply for settlement.

Q.275 What is meant by 'safe third country' and 'links with the United Kingdom'?

A. Where an asylum seeker leaves his country and, during his travel to the United Kingdom, his plane or ship (or any other means of travelling) passes through or lands or calls at a port in a country before arriving in the United Kingdom that person will have to apply for asylum in that country. If it is considered a safe country then asylum will be refused him in the United Kingdom. Where an applicant has escaped to another country he should make his application in that country unless he can show that country is also not a safe place for him. This is a 'third country' application and, unless he can show strong links with the United Kingdom, the applicant will be refused asylum on grounds that his claim is 'without foundation', or is frivolous, as will claims not based on the grounds set out by the UNHCR. Those whose claims have been certified by the

Secretary of State to be 'without foundation' do not have a full right of appeal; all they have is a 'fast-track' appeal which should be lodged within two days to a special adjudicator whose decision as to whether the 'without foundation' certificate is correct is not appealable.

However, the applicant will not be returned to any country if it is not a 'safe country' for him to be returned to – for example, if there is a possibility that he will be sent back from there to the country he escaped from or to his own country if he has well founded fear on the grounds mentioned above. This principle of 'non-refoulement' (non-returning) also applies not only to the country of origin or 'third country' but to any country where he has reason to fear persecution (UNHCR); (*SSHD v Adrian Chiver* (case no. 10758) Appeal no HX/70386 24 March 1994).

Where the 'third country' test is applicable, his application will be considered thoroughly if he has strong links with the United Kingdom – where his spouse is already in the United Kingdom, or he is a minor (under 18) and unmarried and has a parent in the United Kingdom, or he has an unmarried minor child in the United Kingdom. In such instances the person with whom the applicant has such links in the United Kingdom must have had leave to enter or remain or must have been temporarily admitted as an asylum seeker.

Other instances are where the applicant is an elderly or otherwise dependent parent, or, exceptionally, where the applicant is a relative wholly or mainly dependent on the relative in the United Kingdom and there is an absence of support elsewhere. Thus a brother who has siblings in the United Kingdom but who is not dependent on them will not have his case considered even though he may have factors in his favour such as cultural or linguistic links.

A factor which may influence the exercise of discretion is knowledge of language – for example, if he cannot speak the language of the 'third country' but can speak English this would be relevant. Another factor is whether he has more close relatives in the United Kingdom than in the 'third country'.

Yet another factor is his cultural links with the United Kingdom but, as has been pointed out, this must be in addition to other grounds. Those with spouses or parents here who only have exceptional leave to remain will normally be given leave to enter only after four years unless there are compelling exceptional circumstances (*R v SSHD ex parte Muslu* (1993) Imm.A.R. 151).

Q.276 What are the Convention and Protocol relating to the Status of Refugees and which countries are signatories to them?

A.   The United Nations drew up the Convention relating to the legal status of refugees in 1951. The Convention drew up various articles defining the term 'refugee', the obligations of the signatories, administrative measures, and so forth. The Convention of 1951 only dealt with refugee status of those who had already become refugees before 1 January 1951. Because of new refugee situations that had arisen after that date and which may not fall within the scope of the 1951 Convention, it was necessary to have another document signed by participating nations and a Protocol relating to the status of refugees was drawn up recognising the status of refugees both before and after 1951 so as to give them all equal status.

Some states are signatories only to the Convention, others only to the Protocol, and some to both, and the dates on which various countries became signatories vary. It appears that 116 states signed both, four states signed only the Protocol, and three signed only the Convention.

Most of the following have signed both the 1951 Convention and the 1967 Protocol. Over and above this, some states adopted the condition that to be a refugee the events referred to must have occurred in Europe before 1 January 1951, whilst others adopted the condition that the events must have occurred in Europe and elsewhere before 1 January 1951. Those marked (*) signed only the 1951 Convention and those marked (**) only the 1967 Protocol.

Those marked (***) adopted the condition that events must have occurred before 1 January 1951 in Europe. All the others apply the convention without geographical limits. This does not mean they do not accept other refugees. They do, but not under their obligations under the Convention:

Albania; Algeria; Angola; Argentina; Armenia; Australia; Austria; Azerbaijan; Bahamas; Belgium; Belize; Benin; Bolivia; Bosnia-Herzegovenia; Botswana; Brazil (***); Bulgaria; Burkina-faso; Burundi; Cambodia; Cameroon; Canada; Cape Verde (**); Central African Republic; Chad; Chile; China; Colombia; Congo; Costa Rica; Cote d'Ivoire; Croatia; Cyprus; Czech Republic; Denmark; Djibouti; Dominican Republic; Ecuador; Egypt; El Salvador; Equatorial Guinea; Ethiopia; Fiji; Finland; France; Gabon; Gambia; Germany; Ghana; Greece; Guatamala; Guinea; Guinea-Bissau; Haiti; the Holy See; Honduras; Hungary; Iceland; Iran; Ireland; Israel; Italy (***); Jamaica; Japan; Kenya; Korean Republic; Lesotho; Liberia; Liechenstein; Luxembourg; Madagascar (*) (***); Malawi; Mali; Malta (***); Mauritania; Monaco (*)(***); Morocco; Mozambique; Netherlands; New Zealand; Nicaragua; Niger; Nigeria; Norway; Panama; Papua New Guinea; Paraguay (***); Peru; Philippines; Poland; Portugal; Romania; Russian Federation; Rwanda; Samoa (*); Sao Tome and Principé; Senegal; Seychelles; Sierra Leone; Slovak Republic; Slovenia; Somalia; Spain; Sudan; Surinam; Swaziland (**); Sweden; Switzerland; Tanzania; Togo; Tunisia; Turkey(***); Tuvalu; Uganda;

United Kingdom; United States of America (**); Uruguay; Venezuela (**); Yemen; (Yugoslavia); Zaire; Zambia; Zimbabwe.

Q.277 What is the position of those running away from civil war?

A.   The UNHCR states that in cases of grave disturbances involving civil war conditions, or in ethnic clashes, persecution of a specific ethnic group or national group may occur in only one part of the country. In such a situation a person will not be excluded from refugee status 'merely because he could have sought refuge in another part of the same country, if under all the circumstances it would not have been reasonable to expect him to do so.' It is quite a difficult situation and the applicant will have to show that it was not possible to go to the 'safe' part of the country. The current policy, from the case of *Stjepan Curic* (10934), is that the Home Office grants exceptional leave to remain to those from a 'war zone'. Furthermore, where the Home Office has stated a 'policy' not considered within the rules, then it will be held to carry out such policy unless it can show very good reasons for deviating from its policy (*ex parte Benjamin Amankwah* (1994) Imm.A.R. 240; see also question 27).

Violence to individuals flowing from conflict between factions can amount to persecution (*Jeyakumaran* (1994) Imm.A.R. 45) thereby falling within the statement of the UNHCR mentioned above.

Q.278 Can someone with dual nationality seek asylum in the United Kingdom?

A.   Where a person has more than one citizenship then it means he has the protection of each of the countries of which he is a national. This means that if he is in fear of persecution in one country of which he is a national he can go to the other country of which he is also a national and seek protection there. National protection takes precedence over international protection. If the person has British nationality as well as that of the country he is fleeing from he can, of course, enter the United Kingdom as a citizen. If, however, his other citizenship is not British then he is expected to flee from the one country of nationality to his other country of nationality which is considered a safe country for him (*Miller v IAT* (1988) Imm.A.R. 358).

Q.279 Can an asylum seeker, or someone granted refugee status, or other applicants travel abroad?

A.   Yes. Where a person has been granted refugee status he can apply for travel documents from the Home Office to enable him to travel abroad. Usually such documents will be valid for every country except the country from which he fled. Using his national passport or demanding it back from the Home Office may affect his status as a refugee, so it is always advisable to obtain a travel document. This will enable the holder to return to the United Kingdom at any time whilst it is still valid. By visiting his home country the refugee may be deemed to have re-availed himself of his former country's protection and to have lost his refugee status. There are instances when such a visit is necessary and may not result in loss. A refugee who has gained settlement rights (obtained indefinite leave to remain) can travel anywhere but will be subject to the same rules that apply to returning residents (see above).

In the case of someone who has not yet been granted refugee status but has only exceptional leave to remain, he will normally keep his passport. His leave will lapse if he travels outside the United Kingdom and any application to return may have to be considered anew. If he travels to the country from which he fled he may be allowed back within the period of his leave, depending on the reasons for and frequency of his visits, but this may make any further application for extension after the date of his leave seem very suspicious and therefore more difficult. Such a person should keep his passport up-to-date or apply for Home Office travel documents.

Those whose applications for asylum are still under consideration, where no decision to grant exceptional leave to remain or refugee status has been made, have no provisions made for the application for a travel document.

It is important to note that those who make an application of any type (for example, for extension of leave to remain) and who withdraw their passports from the Home Office for the purpose of travelling will be deemed to have withdrawn their application if the withdrawal is made before a decision has been taken. This may result in difficulties, particularly if the leave to remain has expired. Those who request their passports back for other reasons (for example, for identification purposes but not for travelling) will still have any application considered as pending. It is also important to state the reason for asking for the passport back in the letter requesting the return of the passport.

Q.280 Can asylum be transferred from another country to the United Kingdom?

A.   This is possible but is very difficult as authorities do not wish to add to the number of refugees in their country. However, in certain cases where asylum has been granted in one country, and a very convincing case is made for transfer, it may be possible. For instance, where the person has difficulties in that country (with language, culture or harassment by certain groups) or has strong connections with the United Kingdom, or has close relatives, or several relatives, or there is a large ethnic or religious community here to which he belongs, he may be allowed to transfer his status to the United Kingdom.

Chapter 10

Offences and deportation

ILLEGAL ENTRY

Q.281 Is illegal entry an offence?

A.   Under the Immigration Act 1971 there are various offences that can be committed by those with no right to be in the United Kingdom either as citizens, by right of abode, or by leave to enter or remain. Although illegal entry is an offence under the Immigration Act 1971, it is seldom that a person is charged and taken before a court. He can be removed from Britain very quickly and will have no right of appeal in Britain whilst he is here. Illegal entry occurs where a person

   (i) knowingly enters in breach of a deportation order or without leave;

   (ii) having only limited leave, knowingly remains beyond the time limited by such leave, or fails to observe a condition of that leave. He continues to commit an offence throughout any period during which he is in the United Kingdom thereafter and prosecution must take place within six months;

   (iii) having lawfully entered without leave (this pertains to crew members) stays longer than the period allowed him by the Act (namely until the departure of the ship or aircraft);

   (iv) fails to report to a medical officer, or to submit to any tests, without reasonable cause for such failure;

   (v) fails, without reasonable cause, to comply with any restrictions imposed on him relating to residence or reporting to the police or to an immigration officer;

   (vi) disembarks from a ship or aircraft after being put on board for removal from the United Kingdom;

   (vii) embarks contrary to any restrictions placed on him by an order in Council.

A constable or immigration officer can arrest such offenders or suspected offenders without warrant (except for (iv) above). The penalty is a fine of not more than £200 or six months' imprisonment or both. There are certain time limits for prosecution.

Q.282 Who is an 'illegal immigrant'?

A.   Immigration experts say that there is no such person as an 'illegal immigrant' and, despite the fact that this term is in common usage, the correct terminology should be illegal 'entrant'; this is someone whom the immigration officers believe entered the United Kingdom illegally by slipping into the country without being seen or checked at immigration control (*R v Governor of Ashford Remand Centre ex parte Bouzagou* (1983) Imm.A.R. 69) or someone who gained admission to the country by making untruthful statements in order to obtain entry, or someone who is in the United Kingdom in breach of a deportation order, or someone who has breached a condition or time limit of his stay (an 'overstayer').

Such individuals can be removed from the United Kingdom very quickly and have no right of appeal in the United Kingdom until they have left. They may be able to apply to enter if they can satisfy the requirements of the rules. It must be said that a person who enters the United Kingdom without leave because there was no immigration officer to give him leave to enter at the port of entry is an illegal entrant (see *Bouzagou* supra). It is always advisable to check one's passport to see that it has been stamped with leave to enter. If it is not stamped, draw this to the attention of the immigration officer and note what he tells you.

Q.283 What will be the result if deception is used to enter or remain in the United Kingdom?

A.   Deception, if used at any stage, whether to obtain a visa or to remain, will vitiate the person's immigration status even if indefinite leave to remain had been obtained and, as we have seen, the person concerned can be removed from the United Kingdom summarily. Entering clandestinely is just as bad as using fraud or deception or oral or written misrepresentation (*Khawaja v SSHD* [1993] 1 All ER 765). Where no misrepresentation was made by the applicant, illegal entry could not be grounds for a deportation order (*R v SSHD ex parte Annabel Dordas* (1992) Imm.A.R. 99).

There is no general liability to 'undeceive' someone if you did not cause the misapprehension. The deception must play a decisive part in obtaining entry for it stands to reason that if the authorities were not deceived then entry was not obtained by deception. (See below for the difference between removal and deportation.)

Q.284 What may amount to deception?

A.   Non-disclosure of a material fact can be deception – for example, failure to answer a question on previous stays in the United Kingdom can be a non-disclosure of a material fact as can false representation or inaccurate representation. The case of *Khawaja* (1984) AC 74 (HL) places the burden of proof of such non-disclosure on the immigration officer. The intention to deceive is irrelevant. It does not matter whether an individual is unaware that he is entering illegally (*R v SSHD ex parte Abdul Khaled* (1987) Imm.A.R. 67; see also *Bougazou's* case, supra). This would be the case even where the fraud were carried out by a third party without the knowledge of the entrant to Britain. If the immigration officer made a mistake but no fraud has been perpetrated by the entrant, this is not illegal entry (*SSHD ex parte Ram* [1979] 1 All ER 687, *R v IAT ex parte Coomasaru* [1983] 1 WLR 14); but where there was fraud or misrepresentation it is illegal entry (*R v SSHD ex parte Choudry* [1978] 3 All ER 790).

ASSISTING ILLEGAL ENTRY

Q.285 Is it also an offence to assist someone to enter the United Kingdom?

A.   (i) Anyone who knowingly makes arrangements or is concerned with the making of arrangements or in carrying out any arrangements for securing or facilitating the entry in the United Kingdom of anyone he knows to be an illegal entrant is guilty of an offence. If the offence is summarily convicted he can receive a maximum fine of £400 or will receive six months' prison sentence or both, and if convicted on indictment he can receive a fine and/or imprisonment of up to seven years. This offence can be committed by a citizen of the United Kingdom and Colonies and by British subjects without citizenship, citizens, and by one or two other categories, even where the illegal acts are performed outside the United Kingdom. Where a person is convicted on indictment under this offence and he is the owner or one of the owners or a director or manager of a company which is the owner or is the captain of a ship, aircraft, or vehicle, used or intended to be used for carrying out the arrangement in respect of which the offence is committed, the court could order the forfeiture of such ship , aircraft or vehicle subject to certain conditions.

(ii) Anyone knowingly harbouring someone he knows or has reasonable cause to believe, is an illegal entrant, or a person who has committed an offence under (i) above can receive a fine of £400, or six months' imprisonment, or both.

OTHER OFFENCES

Q.286 What other offences are there relating to immigration?

A.   (i) Anyone who without reasonable cause refuses to submit to a medical test;

(ii) fails or refuses, without reasonable excuse, to furnish or produce any information or document in his possession or control which he is required to produce (as provided for in a Schedule to the Act);

(iii) makes any false statement or representation or which he does not believe to be true to an immigration officer or other person lawfully acting in the execution of the Act (see question 28);

(iv) without lawful authority alters any certificate or entry clearance, work-permit, or other documents issued or made under the Act or possesses any of these documents which he knows to be false, or has reasonable cause to believe may be false;

(v) fails to complete or produce, without reasonable cause, a landing or embarkation card in accordance with any order;

(vi) fails, without reasonable cause, to comply with any regulation or order (dealing with registration with the police, registers of hotels, and so forth);

(vii) obstructing an immigration officer or other person lawfully acting in the course of his duties in relation to this Act.

commits a summary offence carrying a penalty of a fine of not more than £200, or six months' imprisonment, or both.

OFFENCES CONNECTED WITH SHIPS/AIRCRAFT/PORTS

Q.287 Are there any offences that carriers are liable to commit?

A.   1.(i) A captain of a ship or aircraft who knowingly and without reasonable excuse permits a person to disembark when required under the Act to prevent it, or fails to take any steps he is required to take, or fails to comply with any directions under the Act for the removal of a person from the United Kingdom;

or

(ii) an owner or agent of a ship or aircraft who arranges, or is knowingly concerned in any arrangements for his ship or aircraft to call at a port other than a port of entry contrary to the Act, or fails without reasonable excuse to take steps to supply the passengers with landing or embarkation cards, or fails without reasonable excuse to make arrangements for the removal of a person from the United Kingdom when required to do so under the Act, or being the owner or agent of the ship or aircraft, or being concerned with the management of a port, fails, without reasonable excuse, to take steps required by the Act in relation to embarkation or disembarkation of passengers where a control area is designated, will be guilty of the offence and on summary conviction will receive a fine of up to £200 or up to six months' imprisonment, or both.

Under the Immigration (Carriers' Liability) Act 1987, any carrier (such as an aircraft or ship) which brings in passengers without proper documents will be liable to pay £2000 or such sum as may be prescribed by the Secretary of State on demand. This is not strictly speaking an 'offence' in the criminal sense but it nevertheless carries heavy penalties. Where a passenger arrives at the port of entry and fails to produce a valid passport with a photograph or some other document establishing nationality or citizenship, or where he is required to obtain a visa for entry and fails to produce one, then the carriers are made to pay unless it can be shown that the passenger had a valid passport and visa at the time of embarkation. Sometimes passengers who are intending to seek asylum tear up their (false) passports or other documents (in some cases obtained through illegal means in order to be able to escape).

DEPORTATION BY COURT RECOMMENDATION

Q.288 Can a court sentence anyone to deportation?

A.   No. The courts (that is the regular courts of law and not the adjudicators) can only recommend deportation and it will be for the Home Secretary to decide whether to deport or not.

Q.289 When does a court recommend deportation?

A.   According to the Immigration Act 1971 the offender recommended for deportation must have been over the age of 17 years and must be convicted of an imprisonable offence of any nature, not necessarily concerning immigration, and any court which has the power to sentence may make the recommendation.

Before making the recommendation the court should give seven days' notice in writing to the offender of its intention before the sentencing. This notice contains a list of those not liable to deportation. Where the court makes a recommendation of deportation but has not sentenced the offender to imprisonment, and he is not on bail, the offender will be detained unless the court orders him not to be detained or the Secretary of State orders his release pending his consideration of the case, or will be placed under a restriction (either residential or involving reporting to the police).

The person who has been through a normal court and has been found guilty of an offence can appeal through the normal court system against his conviction and or sentence. This appeal procedure is not available within the immigration appeal system. Where such an appeal is pending, a deportation order will not be made on the court's recommendation and normally no order will be made until the expiry of the period for an appeal.

DEPORTATION BY THE HOME OFFICE

Q.290 When is someone liable to a Home Office deportation?

A.   The 1971 Act says that a person may be liable to deportation if he has only limited leave to enter or remain and does not comply with any condition attached to his leave, or remains beyond the time granted and becomes an overstayer, or if the Secretary of State deems his deportation necessary for the 'public good', or if another person to whose family he belongs is or has been ordered to be deported. He will also be liable to deportation if he is convicted of a criminal offence and is over the age of 17 and has been recommended for deportation by a court empowered to do so. Where a person recommended for deportation made by a court claims asylum prior to the making of the deportation order, a decision to make a deportation order will then be made so as to enable an appeal to be brought.

Where the decision to deport by the Secretary of State (in normal immigration matters and not through a court recommendation) has been taken, a notice will be sent to the person concerned telling him of this decision to deport and telling him of his rights of appeal (within the immigration appeal system) or of making representations (in cases involving security or political cases). After the issue of such a notice (of his decision to deport) a detention order may be issued. A restriction order is an alternative to the detention order. This relates to place of residence, employment, or occupation, and requires a person to report to the police at given intervals pending a deportation order.

Q.291 Can an appeal be made against deportation?

A.   If the above is the case, the person can appeal to an adjudicator to be released on bail (see below regarding bail). If, after the notice, the person decides to appeal and sends in his appeal within the time allowed for such appeals to be made, then the Home Office will send a summary of the facts of the case and the reason for the decision to deport to the appeals authority which, in turn, will notify the appellant of the arrangements for the hearing.

It is only after an appeal fails or the period for an appeal has lapsed without any appeal being made that a deportation order will be signed. A deportation order can be rescinded by the Secretary of State at any time. Certain people who were granted limited leave to enter (not leave to remain) less than seven years before the decision to deport, and who have failed to observe a condition of their stay (this includes overstaying), have a limited right of appeal against a decision. The same applies to family deportation for breaches of conditions, including overstaying, unless there is no power in law to make the order.

Q.292 Is there anyone who cannot be deported?

A.   Yes. A British citizen or someone with a right of abode may not be deported. The wife or child of a Commonwealth citizen settled in the United Kingdom on 1 January 1973 and, in certain instances, the family of a person who (being the head of the family) is being deported. Under the 1971 Immigration Act (qualified by the 1988

Immigration Act) certain members of a diplomatic mission and their families and members of their household (under the Diplomatic Privileges Act 1964) may not be deported.

A Home Office policy relating to deportation is that where the subject is married to a British citizen or a person settled in the United Kingdom and such marriage is genuine and subsisting and has subsisted for at least two years, and such marriage predates the deportation order or removal order, or where one or more children of such marriage has a right of abode in the United Kingdom, or where the settled spouse has lived in the United Kingdom for a long period and it will be unreasonable to accompany the spouse being deported or removed, then such a person will not be deported or removed.

Q.293 What factors are taken into account before a deportation order is made?

A.   The rules state that the following factors are considered: age, length of residence in the United Kingdom, connections with the United Kingdom, personal history, character, employment record (if any), domestic circumstances, previous criminal record, nature of any offence for which the person has been convicted, compassionate circumstances, representations made on the individual's behalf.

Representation by an immigration adviser can be a powerful element in this regard as he will be able to collate all the relevant facts and present them citing legal cases that support the individual's position.

Even where overstaying occurred, consideration will be given to a claim of long residence and the strength of the person's connection with the United Kingdom, the result of deportation on children, and any other compassionate circumstances, in order to decide the desirability of a deportation order (*Kin-fai Chan and Yuet-ling Chan v SSHD* (15 April 1994) (Appeal no. TH/40655/93)). Where there has been illegal entry, deportation action is not normally activated where the person is genuinely married to a spouse settled in the United Kingdom and the marriage is subsisting, but in such cases the marriage must have been in existence before any action to deport is commenced and the marriage has been in existence for at least two years. Where the marriage has not been in existence for that long then consideration may be given to where the spouse has lived in the United Kingdom from a very early age and it will be unreasonable to have the settled spouse accompany the spouse to be deported or removed or where there is a child of the marriage with a right of abode in the United Kingdom.

A common-law spouse's deportation will be considered in the same way. Those who have been in the United Kingdom for more than seven years also have a stronger chance of having a deportation order cancelled on appeal.

Q.294 Can anything be done after an appeal has failed but before the order to deport is made?

A.   The only other action a person can take is to make it known to the Home Office that he is prepared to leave the United Kingdom immediately without a deportation order being made and that (where this is possible) he will pay his own fares. He will be in a slightly better position later on if no deportation order has been made. Alternatively, he may notify the Home Office of his intention to leave without a deportation order and ask for a supervised departure – where the fares are paid and he is put on board an aircraft or ship and sent back.

Q.295 When the head of a family is deported will every other member of the family also be deported?

A.   The 1971 Act gives the Home Secretary certain rights to deport family members as well as the head of the family. Where a decision to deport a family member has been made, the Secretary of State will notify the member of his decision and of the right of appeal. The notice will also give the member the option of leaving voluntarily without appealing or after his appeal fails. (This option should be considered after consultation with advisers if the person wishes to remain.) The family members to be deported with the head of the family are to be named in the order at the outset or within a certain period of time otherwise the order against such family members cannot be carried out (1971 Act). The wife of a deportee will not normally be deported if:

(a) she has qualified for settlement in her own right; or

(b) she has been living apart from the deportee.

The Home Office will take into consideration all the above as well as whether the wife has the ability to maintain herself and her children (if any) or whether she can be maintained by relatives or friends without recourse to public funds for the foreseeable future (as opposed to for a short while). The child of a deportee will not normally be deported if:

(a) he and his mother are living apart from the deportee;

(b) the child has spent some time in the United Kingdom and is nearing the age of 18 years;

(c) he has left home and has established himself on an independent basis;

(d) he has married before deportation became a prospect.

The Home Office will consider, in addition to the above, whether the child is of school-going age and the effect of the removal of the child from his education and the practicability of any plans for the child's care and maintenance in the United Kingdom if both his parents are removed. Any representations made on behalf of the wife or child or both will be considered.

Generally, if a deportation order will substantially affect a third party it will be given grave consideration by the Home Office or on appeal (*ex parte Dhunna* (1992) Imm.A.R. 457).

Q.296 What happens after a deportation order has been signed?

A.   The person may be removed from the United Kingdom very quickly. He will be returned to the country of which he is a national or which provided him with travel documents. The deportee may be able to show that, apart from these two places, there is another country that will accept him. The deportee can, however, only appeal against the named country to which he is to be deported. If he returns to the United Kingdom whilst the deportation is still in effect he may be removed under the same order depending on the circumstances.

Q.297 Can a deportation order be revoked?

A.   Yes. The rules provide for revocation of a deportation order if an application is made. The normal period before an application for revocation will be considered is three years unless there are exceptional circumstances. In the case of serious criminal offences the exclusion period can be longer. The application may be made to an entry clearance officer in the applicant's country or directly to the Home Office in the United Kingdom. The circumstances under which revocation will be considered are receipt of representations regarding: the grounds on which the order was made; any new information in support of revocation (for example information coming to light which was not available to either the court making the recommendation or the appellate authorities where an appeal was lodged, or information regarding a change of circumstances since the order was made); the interest of the community (including maintenance of effective immigration control); and the interests of the applicant (including compassionate circumstances).

Where an application is made for revocation and it is refused, the decision will be notified with a notice of the applicant's right of appeal. There is a right of appeal to an adjudicator. Where the order was made against a member of a family, the appeal lies directly to the Tribunal. The applicant cannot appeal whilst in Britain, nor where the exclusion was based on the personal decision of the Secretary of State on the grounds that the order was conducive to public good.

Where a person re-enters the United Kingdom after a deportation order has been enforced and has not been revoked, he will be an illegal entrant even if he obtained entry clearance by some means – such clearance is not an implied revocation (*Watson v I.O. (Gatwick Airport)* (1986) Imm. A.R. 75). Even where a deportation order is revoked, this does not entitle him to enter without entry clearance.

Q.298 What is the difference between deportation and removal?

A. Under a deportation the deportee is served with an order, signed by the Home Secretary, for him to be sent away from the United Kingdom. This normally occurs where the person was initially in the country legally but later breached a condition of his leave to enter (for example, by taking employment when prohibited to do so) or has overstayed his period of leave, or has been convicted of a serious criminal offence has been recommended for deportation.

Removals take place where, technically, the person to be removed has not been granted leave to enter legally. In other words such a person is an illegal entrant (see questions 281–284) and he can be removed from the United Kingdom summarily.

BAIL

Q.299 When is bail given?

A. Under the 1971 Act a person who has been detained for more than seven days after his arrival, without any decision being made to grant or refuse him admission, may apply for bail. Once a decision has been made under the provisions of the Act (para. 22 of Schedule 2) the person has no right to bail on this ground (*Nadarajah Vilvarajah* (1990) Imm.A.R. 457). A person who has been detained pending removal or deportation and who has a valid 'in-country' appeal pending against a decision to refuse him entry or against removal as an illegal entrant or because he has entered against a deportation order, or is appealing against the destination named in the order to remove or deport him, can apply for bail (para. 29 of Schedule 2).

Q.300 Who may grant bail?

A.   The immigration officer dealing with the case may grant bail and it is advisable to apply to him for bail. A police officer of the rank of inspector and above may also approve bail. An adjudicator before whom a case is pending may grant bail.

It should be noted that the Bail Act 1976 does not generally apply to immigration cases (but see also The Supreme Court Act 1981 s16 as to appeals to the Court of Appeal and to the High Court).

The Act, however, specifies one instance in which bail is mandatory (subject to certain exceptions). Bail must be granted where an appellant has appealed to the Tribunal or where leave to appeal has been granted.

Q.301 How is bail applied for?

A.   Bail can be applied for orally or in writing and may be in a very simple form 'the appellant/applicant applies for bail so as to be at liberty pending the appeal and will abide by all the conditions set' is sufficient. The appellant/applicant must give his full name, detention address, any amount that he can offer in security for bail, and the names, addresses, and occupations of two persons who are willing to act as sureties. The application, if made in writing, must be signed by the appellant/applicant. It is advisable for the sureties to be present at the application if it is made before an adjudicator. The sureties present at the application can be different from those named before as it is their undertaking that is important. Evidence of financial means, fixed addresses, degree of contact, knowledge of, and relationship with the appellant or applicant will be essential, and so will the sureties' character, criminal record, immigration record, marital status, and parental status.

In some cases the appellant/applicant may be absent when the date for the application comes up. The adjudicator may authorise the governor of the detention centre to take the details from the appellant/applicant and the CIO or police inspector to take the details of the sureties. These instructions are endorsed on the file. Forms are filled in, depending on whether the application is made under the 'seven-day decision rule' or the 'appeal pending rule' as mentioned in question 299 above.

Q.302 Can bail be opposed?

A.   Yes. In cases where bail is opposed it is based on one or more of the following grounds: that the appellant/applicant will not answer to bail, or has previously failed to comply with bail conditions, or is likely to commit an offence if released, or is likely to be a danger to public health, or that the time left for him to be held before the appeal hearing is quite short, or that he is suffering from a mental disorder and detention is necessary for his own or any other person's protection, or that the appellant/applicant is under 17 years and no satisfactory arrangements have been made for his care. Where the adjudicator indicates willingness to grant bail, the Home Office Presenting Officer will be given time to examine the sureties and to state his reasons (if any) to the adjudicator for opposing bail if the details of the sureties are unsatisfactory. The appellant will be given the opportunity to refute these grounds.

Q.303 If bail is granted, what next?

A. The adjudicator will fix the sum, which is normally £1000 per surety but may be as high as £5000 in total. Residential restrictions may be imposed and there may be a requirement for the person concerned to report to the police. These conditions are normally requested by the Home Office Presenting Officer. After the file has been endorsed and the formalities have been completed, the appellant/applicant will be let out to return to court on a date specified for his appeal. Where bail is granted pending an appeal, and the appeal is withdrawn, the bail will be withdrawn. Where a person has applied for bail and decides to leave the country voluntarily before a deportation order is served on him, he should notify the Home Office well in advance of this so as to avoid any difficulties that may result to the sureties because, theoretically, leaving the country will make the sureties liable.

Q.304 Can a person let out on bail be arrested?

A. Yes. An immigration officer or a police officer of any rank may arrest anyone released on bail without a warrant if he has reasonable grounds to believe that the person is likely to break the conditions to appear at a place and time specified in the terms of his bail, or that he is breaking or has broken any condition, or if such officer is notified in writing by any surety that the surety has reason to believe that the person released is not likely appear as specified and therefore wishes to be relieved as surety. The officer may obtain a search warrant to allow him to enter any premises (forcibly if need be) to search for and arrest the person concerned. This power of arrest applies whether the bail was granted due to failure to reach a decision to admit or refuse entry or to an appeal pending, even though such powers are given under separate paragraphs of the Schedule in the Immigration Act.

Chapter 11

Appeals

Q.305 Who has the right to plead before the adjudicators or tribunal?

A.   The person who is appealing can do so by himself without a representative, solicitor, or barrister. If, however, he wants someone else to appear for him, this can be done by a friend or a representative who is either a solicitor, a barrister, or an immigration counsellor. The hearing is quite informal, unlike in a court of law. The parties remain seated whilst addressing the panel or the adjudicator. The person can call witnesses. Rules of admissibility of evidence that normally operate in the courts of law are not applied strictly. All relevant evidence is admissible although some will carry less weight (for example hearsay evidence where original evidence could practicably have been provided but only photocopies are produced). Letters headed 'to whom it may concern' may also not carry much weight. Submissions of 'no case' are not made by the Home Office Presenting Officer. Costs are not awarded in these appeals.

Q.306 Are there people who have no right of appeal?

A.   Yes. There are certain people who have no right of appeal: visitors, prospective students and other short-term applicants (for under six months) cannot appeal against refusal of entry clearance or a visa abroad, nor can they appeal against refusal of entry on arrival.

The rules do not permit certain categories (such as visitors) to have their leave to stay extended and those who apply under such categories to have their leave extended, even outside the rules, will be refused and an appeal is not available.

Illegal entrants cannot appeal under the immigration appeals system but may apply for judicial review.

Those from visa countries who arrive at the airport without a visa and apply here for entry and are refused also may not appeal.

There is no appeal against a refusal to grant an application made outside the rules where there is discretion to grant or refuse.

There is no right of appeal against the refusal of a work permit.

There is no appeal where the Secretary of State has himself certified that the person's entry is not conducive to the public good on grounds of national security, but there is a non-statutory procedure whereby the question is referred to three advisers appointed by the Secretary of State.

There is no appeal where a visitor from a visa country wishes to switch to student status and is refused.

A person from a non-Commonwealth country who applies as a working holidaymaker will be refused with no right of appeal.

In asylum cases where the Home Office has certified that an application is 'without foundation' there is a 'fast-track' appeal to a special adjudicator but there is no appeal where the special adjudicator upholds the decision of 'without foundation'.

The Immigration Act 1988 reduced the full right of appeal where a person is being deported for overstaying or in breach of a condition. The only argument that may be allowed on appeal is that the person concerned has not overstayed or breached his conditions of stay. This may be a difficult allegation to counter as it would be ludicrous for the Home Office to make a decision to deport unless it has firm evidence of overstaying or breaches of conditions. The same applies to those whose stay have been less than seven years and are being deported (*ex parte Fuller* (1993) Imm.A.R. 177).

Q.307 Where there is a right of appeal, how long will the appellant have to bring the appeal?

A.   Where the appellant is outside the country and wants to appeal from abroad, the normal period allowed is three months from the date of the decision in an appeal to an adjudicator and, after that, 42 days in an appeal to the Tribunal.

In those cases where an individual is refused entry whilst holding a visa or entry clearance, or even a work permit, then he may appeal within 28 days from the date of refusal in the United Kingdom. Appeals to the Tribunal must be within 14 days. Those from non-visa countries who are refused entry have 28 days; those named in a deportation order (such as illegal entrants) who are appealing against the order either on the grounds that they are not the persons named in the order or that the Secretary of State has exceeded his powers in making the order have 28 days and may appeal to the Tribunal. They are only allowed 14 days if they are still in the United Kingdom. If they have been removed from the country, they have 28 days to appeal to the adjudicator and, after that, they have 42 days to appeal to the Tribunal.

The same time limits as mentioned in the above paragraph apply in an appeal against revocation of a deportation order.

Those who are seeking asylum and have been refused on grounds that the application is not well founded would use a 'fast-track' appeal process – they have two days to appeal (not including Saturdays,

Sundays and public holidays) if they are served personally with the refusal otherwise, where the refusal is sent to their detention centre or to their address, they have 10 working days.

Other asylum seekers who are refused have 10 working days to appeal to the special adjudicator. For asylum refusal appeals to the Tribunal (if the adjudicator refuses an appeal) the period is five days. Appeals to the Tribunal from abroad is 42 days. In most other cases the period for an appeal is 14 days from the date of the decision.

It is always advisable to send in the appeal even if it is out of time. The adjudicators or special adjudicators will normally allow the appeal to proceed. The time limit in Tribunal appeals must be strictly observed.

Leave must be obtained before an appeal can be lodged with the Tribunal and it is essential that the grounds are carefully drafted. These grounds can be served later provided that notice that they will follow is given at the time of the appeal and that a general ground for appeal is mentioned.

In most cases the notice of appeal must be in writing but, where a person has arrived at the airport/port and is refused entry, he can request an appeal orally.

Q.308 What are the stages of appeal?

A.   A decision by the IO or the ECO or the Home Office can be appealed by the adjudicator, or in asylum cases to the appeal adjudicator. From there an appeal may lie to the Immigration Appeals Tribunal and (with leave from the Tribunal or, failing that, with leave from the Court of Appeal) to either have a judicial review (see question 32 above) or to go to the Court of Appeal.

Before July 1993, an appeal went to the court for a judicial review (with leave). Since then s. 9 of the Asylum and Immigration Appeals Act 1993 takes an appeal from the Tribunal to the Court of Appeal directly but only on a question of law and not of fact.

The decision appealed against must be a final decision. This section clarifies Part 2 of the Immigration Act 1971 which refers to appeals 'to an appropriate court'. It follows that where the appeal is granted on a question of illegality or irrationality (under what is referred to by lawyers as the Wednesbury Rules – *Associated Provincial Picture Houses Ltd. v Wednesbury Corporation* [1948] 1 KB 223) an 'arguable point of law' exists and therefore goes to the Court of Appeal rather than for a judicial review as was previously the case (*Edwards v Bairstow* [1955] All.E.R. 175). If the decision of the Tribunal is not a final decision (e.g. refusal of leave) then there is no appeal to the Court of Appeal.

Chapter 12

British nationality

OBTAINING BRITISH NATIONALITY

Q.309 Does having indefinite leave to remain make a person a British citizen?

A. No. This question was briefly answered above in question 14. Having indefinite leave to remain means what it says – the person concerned may remain. This does not involve a change of citizenship. The person may become a resident permanently and may stay for the rest of his life here but will not become a British citizen automatically without applying for it and satisfying certain conditions. Obtaining settlement status, however, is an essential step in obtaining citizenship.

Q.310 Can a person become a British citizen and still keep his original nationality?

A. Yes. The United Kingdom allows dual nationality. The danger is that if an individual is a national of a country that does not permit dual citizenship he stands the chance of losing his original status and, as a result, losing certain rights that he may have had (such as the right to hold freehold land in that country).

Another disadvantage is that whilst an individual holds both a British passport and another country's passport he cannot be afforded diplomatic protection by the British Embassy (or High Commission) against the State whose nationality that person also holds when he is in that other State, due to the Master Nationality Rule under international law.

Q.311 Which law governs British citizenship?

A. The British Nationality Act 1981, which came into operation on 1 January 1983, made very substantial changes in nationality law. No longer will those born in the United Kingdom have automatic British nationality. The concept of citizenship through place of birth (*jus soli*) was replaced by that of citizenship through parentage (*jus sanguinis*).

Thus it is important to have a parent who is either a British citizen or one who is settled in the United Kingdom. This does not mean that those with citizenship ('patrials') before this Act lost it. It set down new criteria for obtaining citizenship from 1983.

A 'patrial' was born in the United Kingdom or adopted in the United Kingdom; or had a father who was born or adopted in the United Kingdom or was registered or naturalised in the United Kingdom before the patrial was born; or was registered or naturalised in the United Kingdom because of his residence in the United Kingdom.

A woman, who was a citizen of the United Kingdom and colonies but who was married to a United Kingdom citizen before October 1971, and was registered as such, or was at any time married to a patrial, or had lived in the United Kingdom for five years and became settled before 1 January 1983. All patrials had the right of abode. The Act created three new types of citizenship: British citizenship, British overseas citizenship, and British dependent territories citizenship.

If, on 31 January 1983, you were a patrial (with general right of abode) you would have become a British citizen.

If you were a citizen of the United Kingdom and colonies but not a patrial, but the colony concerned was independent on 1 January 1983 (for example Sierra Leone, Malaysia, and so forth) you would have become a British overseas citizen. If the colony was not yet independent on that date (Hong Kong being an example) you became a British dependent citizen.

Q.312 What is a British overseas citizen?

A. A BOC is a person who was born in a country that was a British colony but who did not qualify for citizenship of that country at independence, or of any other country, and therefore retained his British nationality. This does not mean that such a person is a British citizen. Anyone who was a citizen of the United Kingdom and colonies immediately before 1 January 1983 became a BOC automatically on that date if he did not then acquire British citizenship or British dependent territories citizenship. This status is not generally transmissible. There is no provision for acquisition of British overseas citizenship by birth, adoption, naturalisation, or descent. A BOC who has been present in the United Kingdom for five years since 1 January 1983 becomes eligible for registration as a British citizen.

A child can be registered as such only under very exceptional circumstances provided by the British Nationality Act 1981, but the requirements are about the same as those for naturalisation and thus it may be advisable to apply for the latter. BOCs may not have the right of readmission if they are absent for two years and will be subject to the same rules as returning residents but, if they have lived in Britain for most of their lives but have stayed away longer than two years, they will be allowed to return.

BOCs who have no other country to go to will not be deported although pressure may be put on those who may have another country that they can go to (for example those with dual nationality) to leave voluntarily. Where a BOC can be admitted into another country if a visa is applied for, he can be deported to such a country (*R v SSHD ex parte Patel* (1993) Imm.A.R 392, *R v SSHD ex parte Sunsara* (1995) Imm.A.R. 15).

Some countries do not accept duality of citizenship and will not allow such persons to go there freely (*in re Kinnare* 11879) In that case removal or deportation may not be effected. If exceptional leave to remain is requested, the applicant will be granted one year and this may be extended from year to year.

Q.313 Has a British overseas citizen the right of abode in the United Kingdom?

A. No. He needs entry clearance if he is from a visa country or if he wants to enter in certain categories, and he is subject to immigration laws (see above).

Q.314 What is a British protected person (BPP)?

A. A BPP is one who was born in a country which used to be a British protectorate (as distinct from a colony) and who did not gain citizenship of that country or any other country when the protectorate gained independence. For example Sierra Leone was both a colony and a protectorate (Freetown and the present Western Area and certain other small areas formed the colony and the rest of the country was administered as a protectorate). On attaining independence in 1961, those born in the colony who did not qualify for citizenship as mentioned above became British overseas citizens, and those born in the protectorate became British protected persons. Although nominally British subjects, they are not British citizens. Nor are they foreigners, or classed as Commonwealth citizens. They need entry clearance to enter United Kingdom if they are coming into the United Kingdom in any category for which entry clearance is necessary.

Q.315 What are the means by which British citizenship can now be obtained?

A. The Act set down three ways:

(i) by birth in the United Kingdom;

(ii) by naturalisation;

(iii) by registration.

Each of these has its own requirements.

Q.316 What are the requirements to obtain citizenship by birth?

A.   No one becomes a British citizen solely by reason of being born in the
United Kingdom. He can only acquire this status if at least one of his
parents is British or is settled in the United Kingdom. If the child is
illegitimate, only the mother's nationality at time of birth will matter
but, where a child born out of wedlock is legitimised by the subsequent
marriage of the parents, then he is treated as legitimate from the date
of the marriage if the father's domicile permitted legitimation. Where
a child is born outside the United Kingdom after 1 January 1983, if
any one of his parents was born in the United Kingdom or was
registered or naturalised in the United Kingdom before the child's
birth, the child is a British citizen by descent. If a child born outside
the United Kingdom had neither parent born in the United Kingdom,
if they are British citizens such a child will be a citizen by descent.
Where a child is born in the United Kingdom on or after 1 January
1983, with neither of his parents being British or settled at time of
birth, it may be possible to register such a child as British before he
becomes 18 years old if at least one parent subsequently becomes
British or is settled in Britain. Where the child mentioned above has
parents who do not become British or do not settle, then such a child
can be registered after 10 years continuous residence in the United
Kingdom provided he has not been absent for more than 90 days in
each of those 10 years. (This requirement has some flexibility and
where there is good reason for exceeding the days of absence in each
year this will be taken into account.) There are variations in the basis
for citizenship and they cannot all be mentioned here. Those in doubt
about their nationality should seek further advice.

Q.317 What are the requirements for naturalisation?

A.   There are requirements for:

(i) those married to British citizens; and

(ii) others.

Someone married to a British citizen must have been in the United Kingdom legally for at least three years. He must have been granted settlement status before the date he makes his application (irrespective of how short a time this may be). During the three-year period in which he was settled he should not have been absent from the United Kingdom for more than 270 days in total and he must not have been absent from the United Kingdom for more than 90 days in the year before making the application.

He will have to have two referees to sign a form showing that they have known him for a certain number of years (at least two); they must not be related to the applicant nor may they be his solicitors or agents. He should be of good character and should intend to live in the United Kingdom. A fee of £135 is payable at the time of making the application. He should be in the United Kingdom on the date the application is received in the Home Office and should have been present in the United Kingdom on the same date three years before.

For someone not married to a British citizen the qualifications are that he must have lawfully resided in the United Kingdom for at least five years and must have been settled for at least one year before the date of application. He must not have been absent from the United Kingdom for more than 90 days in the year before he applies and must not have been absent for longer than 450 days in total (including the period for the last year) over the five years. He must be of good character, speak English, Welsh or Gaelic passably, and he must intend to live in the United Kingdom. The fee is £170.

A married couple, living in the same address, applying together (if both qualify) will pay only one set of fees and payment must accompany the application.

Where a spouse in this category makes an application and has a spouse who has been in the United Kingdom for only three years (but who has also settled here) it may be advantageous to make one application. Each spouse will then have to fill in a separate form but these forms will be sent together as a joint application and it may be that the application of the spouse of five years will be considered first. If this application is granted, then the application of the spouse who has been in the country for less than five years will be considered as being an application from the spouse of a British citizen and the second spouse may be deemed to be an applicant under category (1) above.

It takes about nine to 16 months for the process in either case to be completed. A visit to the applicant's home by the police or some authorised person may be expected to verify one or two aspects of the answers in the form. Naturalisation is not a right, and the Home Secretary can refuse an application without giving any reasons and such a refusal is not subject to judicial review. The applicant must be in the United Kingdom when the application is received in the Home

Office and should have been present in the United Kingdom on the same date five years before.

Q.318 When an application for naturalisation has been approved is a passport then sent to the applicant?

A.   No. What the applicant will receive is a form containing an oath of allegiance to be sworn and returned. This will then be followed by a certificate of naturalisation. This should be kept in a safe place; if it is lost the Home Office will not issue a replacement certificate. The applicant may be able to obtain a letter from the Home Office. If the applicant wants a passport he should obtain a form from the Post Office nearest to his place of residence. The form for an adult is different from that of a child.

The applicant then presents the completed form with the certificate of naturalisation and any other document requested by the agency as well as the appropriate fees. He will receive a passport within a few days. The new passport is likely to be maroon coloured and smaller than the old blue passports. The applicant must ensure the certificate of naturalisation is returned to him for safe keeping.

Q.319 How does one qualify for registration?

A.   This depends on whether the applicant is under or over 18 years old. If the applicant is under 18 we have seen instances where registration can take place in the answer to question 303 above.

A child found abandoned in the United Kingdom will be presumed to be British at birth. A person under 18 born outside the United Kingdom may be registered if his father or mother was a British citizen by descent and the three of them are or were in Britain at the commencement of the three year period preceding the making of the application, and if none of them has been absent from the United Kingdom for more than 270 days during that three year period, and if both parents consent to the registration. In such a case where the child is illegitimate, only the mother's citizenship by descent will be considered. Where only one parent is alive then that parent's consent is sufficient. The child becomes a British citizen (not by descent) and can transmit citizenship to his children born abroad (which cannot be done if he were a citizen by descent).

There are other variations for the registration of children and if a full list of such grounds is required consultation with an expert in this field should be sought.

In the case of adults, British overseas citizens, British dependent territories citizens, British protected persons, British subjects, and

British nationals (overseas) are all entitled to register if they have been in the United Kingdom for five years and have been settled for one year and have not been absent from the United Kingdom for more than 450 days in total and 90 days in the year prior to application. It is similar to naturalisation but only the categories mentioned can register whilst the others have to naturalise.

Another set of citizens who could have registered was Commonwealth citizens settled in the United Kingdom before 1 January 1973 and who were still minors (under 18) on 1 January 1983 (in other words those born since 1964 who settled before 1 January 1973) and who applied for registration within five years of their eighteenth birthday. This no longer applied after 1987 but the Home Secretary has the discretion to allow registration in certain cases.

Registration as a citizen is a right if the statutory conditions are met, and where it is refused this can be challenged in court. The applicant must be in the United Kingdom when the Home Office receives his application.

Q.320 What if the absence from United Kingdom of an applicant who applies for either naturalisation or registration is longer than allowed?

A. The Home Office has a discretion to waive requirements concerning periods of absence. In considering such a waiver, however, it is possible for the Home Office to take account of the country or countries that the applicant visited during such absence and this may adversely affect the discretion, particularly if such visits raise questions of loyalty or security.

Q.321 What was a British visitor's passport?

A. Anyone resident in the United Kingdom, irrespective of the type of British nationality he possesses, was able to obtain a form from a post office and could apply for this passport. It was valid for one year. The holder could only visit western Europe with this passport. It did not entitle the holder to re-enter without question. Immigration officers did not accept this passport as evidence of the right to re-enter as such a passport was not evidence of British nationality (*R v IAT ex parte Minta* (1992) Imm A.R. 380).

This type of passport was discontinued on 1 January 1996.

Postscript

Due to the increase in 'marriages of convenience' (whereby entrants go through a fake marriage with a British citizen solely for the purpose of fooling the immigration authorities in order to gain settlement rights) there has been an outcry against allowing marriages by those with only limited leave to remain in the country (such as visitors, students and other categories that have to leave the country at the end of the period granted to them). Pressure is being applied to the Home Secretary to prevent such marriages by creating rules that will require such persons to leave the country and to apply for entry from abroad specifically for the purpose of getting married. It will not be surprising if such a rule is passed in the near future and anyone with only limited leave to remain and contemplating marriage here should check this.

In fact it is always wise to check with an immigration adviser at all stages on any matter involving immigration. It may cost a little more, but the expenditure may turn out to be a good investment.

A new development relates to changes in the social benefits claimable by asylum seekers. As from 5 February 1996 the Social Security (Persons from Abroad) Miscellaneous Amendments Regulations 1996 came into effect. These regulations remove the right of claiming income support, housing benefits and council tax benefits from certain asylum seekers, the main group affected. Not all such persons will be caught, however.

Those who applied for asylum after they had entered the country and not immediately upon arrival at the airport or port of entry will, as from that date, be refused the benefits mentioned. Those whose initial asylum applications are refused, even if made at the point of entry, will also lose benefits as soon as the decisions to refuse asylum are made. Those whose applications have been turned down and are awaiting appeal results will no longer be able to claim benefits.

The regulations will not affect those who apply for asylum at the airport or port or point of entry immediately on arrival and they will continue until a decision is given refusing the application. An adverse decision will result in loss of benefits and this position will continue even during an appeal until the decision is given.

Those who come from countries which the Home Office declares are 'upheaval countries' and who apply within three months of such declaration will receive benefits. Those who are asylum seekers before the date of the regulations will not be affected and will continue to receive benefits until decisions are taken on their applications but may become so if they become new claimants of benefits, for instance where they were working and lost their jobs, or lost their homes. Those with refugee status, or those granted exceptional leave to remain, will not lose benefits.

A lot of opposition to this regulation and to two proposed Bills now going through Parliament – the Asylum & Immigration Bill and the Housing Bill –

has been registered and a case is pending against the refusal of benefits under the regulations. It is a pessimistic state for asylum seekers and others as, in addition to not having benefits, one of the Bills mentioned, if passed, will make it an offence for employers to employ foreigners without checking their credentials.

Another development that has taken place is that, since the end of February 1996, the common-law spouse concessions to which questions 252 refers, have been abolished. Now, any foreign national applying to either join a partner or to remain with a partner as a cohabitee should expect to be refused and deportation may result. Where it comes to this stage, then any of the grounds that will make deportation not appropriate may be considered. See question 293.